Praise for Capital Allocators

Through his podcast, Ted has talked with the best investment minds in the world. *Capital Allocators* assembles this collective wisdom into an incredible guidebook for anyone who wants to be truly thoughtful about long-term investing.

– Raphael Arndt, CEO, Australia Future Fund

Capital Allocators is jam-packed with actionable advice from the world's leading investment experts on topics ranging from interviewing managers to decision-making. Ted distills the wisdom of his impressive array of podcast guests into a compendium that deserves highlighting on every page. Take it from me, choosing to read *Capital Allocators* is a good decision.

– Annie Duke, former professional poker player,
best-selling author, and decision strategist

Ted Seides has achieved a remarkable book that draws on the expertise and experience of a broad cross-section of industry leaders. He expertly distills interviews that he conducted directly into a book that seamlessly covers executive, leadership and investment skills and lessons. *Capital Allocators* is a well-crafted and informative read for existing and prospective investment professionals as well as for those who work with the investment industry in any capacity.

– Gregory J. Fleming, President & CEO,
Rockefeller Capital Management

A fantastically broad, deep guide to the asset allocator's world. I wish it had been written 25 years ago. The quotations in it are alone worth the price. You can quote me on that.

– Andrew Golden, CIO, Princeton University
Investment Management Company (PRINCO)

Ted understands the nuance of investment management better than anyone I know, because he's talked to more investors than anyone I know. It's been said that books don't change minds; sentences do. There are so many good lines in this book it's hard to put down.

– Morgan Housel, Partner at Collaborative Fund and best-selling author

Unlike many 'invest like the best' books, *Capital Allocators* does not pretend there is some magical trick that will turn anyone into an investing genius. Instead, Ted Seides details how great investors do the hard work that leads to better outcomes. You won't get rich quick reading this book, but if you take the time to really understand the lessons it teaches, you will be a better, more thoughtful investor.

– Ben Inker, Head of Asset Allocation, GMO

Capital Allocators is an excellent collection of toolkits and frameworks for investing that reflect both the institutions and the different styles of their CIOs. *Capital Allocators* is a starting manual for all the things aspiring CIOs need to consider as they develop their style and strategic vision. Importantly, Ted acknowledges that there are many ways to be a successful CIO and that CIOs can learn from each other in that diversity of viewpoints.

– Ana Marshall, CIO, William and Flora Hewlett Foundation

The world of institutional investing needed Ted's voice – it just didn't know it yet. With this book, and with his unparalleled podcast, Ted has brought a whole hidden world to a broader audience, and anyone interested in how the world's most prominent investors move money is better for it.

– Kip McDaniel, Editor-in-Chief, *Institutional Investor*

Ted has made the world of capital allocation approachable for everyone across hundreds of conversations. Now he's further distilled the lessons into a package that will make any investor better at what they do. Required reading.

– Patrick O'Shaughnessy, CEO, O'Shaughnessy Asset Management

This book boils down the most interesting insights and important lessons from the biggest and most powerful investors on earth – the ones that literally put the capital in capitalism. It offers a glimpse into the thinking of capital allocators in a coherent and digestible format. It should be required reading for anybody interested in investing and certainly will be for my students!

– Ashby H. B. Monk, PhD, Executive Director, Global Projects Center, Stanford University

Page by page, Ted Seides' *Capital Allocators* brings us tools, frameworks and a rich collection of wisdom captured from his professional network. Ted's book allows us to discover how successful CIOs incorporate various aspects of the investment process and lessons learned in navigating financial markets. This book should be mandatory for any investment teams aspiring to evolve and win.

– Mario Therrien, Head of Investment Funds and External Management, Caisse de dépôt et placement du Québec

I have learned something from every podcast, and this book pulls them all together. There is no one right way to be a CIO, we are all unique, but there are still lessons that we can learn from one another and value that comes from understanding the nuances among us. Thank you, Ted, for providing a forum for CIOs to share ideas and for writing this great collection of highlights.

– James Williams, CIO, J. Paul Getty Trust

CAPITAL ALLOCATORS

CAPITAL ALLOCATORS

How the world's elite money
managers lead and invest

TED SEIDES

Harriman House Ltd
3 Viceroy Court
Bedford Road
Petersfield
Hampshire
GU32 3LJ
GREAT BRITAIN
Tel: +44 (0)1730 233870
Email: enquiries@harriman-house.com
Website: harriman.house

First published in 2021.

Hardback ISBN: 978-0-85719-886-0
eBook ISBN: 978-0-85719-887-7

British Library Cataloguing in Publication Data
A CIP catalogue record for this book can be obtained from the British Library.

For the virtuous circle of guests and listeners
on the Capital Allocators *podcast*

And especially for my wife Vanessa,
whose enthusiastic support from the
front row seat lights up the stage

Every owner of a physical copy of this edition of

CAPITAL ALLOCATORS

can download the eBook for free direct from us at Harriman House, in a format that can be read on any eReader, tablet or smartphone.

Simply head to:

ebooks.harriman-house.com/capitalallocators

to get your free eBook now.

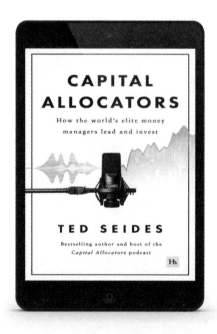

Contents

PART 3: NUGGETS OF WISDOM

APPENDICES

About the Author

Ted Seides, CFA has spent 25 years as an institutional investor, allocating money to managers. He started in 1992 at the Yale University Investments Office, seven years after David Swensen arrived at Yale. Ted spent five years learning under David's tutelage and departed to attend Harvard Business School shortly before David wrote the bible in the industry, *Pioneering Portfolio Management*.

Ted spent a summer job and two years after business school investing directly at three of Yale's managers, hedge fund Brahman Capital, and private equity firms Stonebridge Partners and J.H. Whitney & Company. He learned that life inside the sausage factory is rarely as clean as the final product appears.

He returned to investing through managers in 2002, co-founding and serving as President and Co-Chief Investment Officer of Protégé Partners. Protégé was a leading multibillion-dollar alternative investment firm that invested in and seeded small hedge funds. In 2010, Larry Kochard and Cathleen Rittereiser profiled Ted in the book *Top Hedge Fund Investors*, and in 2016 Ted authored *So You Want to Start a Hedge Fund: Lessons for Managers and Allocators* to share lessons from his experience.

On a slow day in 2007, Ted had the bright idea to challenge a statement made by Warren Buffett about the superiority of index funds over hedge funds. With aspirations to demonstrate the value of hedge funds to institutional portfolios, he initiated a charitable wager with Warren that pitted the 10-year performance of the S&P 500 against a selection of five hedge fund of funds from 2008–2017. Protégé Partners lost the bet, and Ted still wonders about the probability distribution of outcomes and the quality of his decision process.

In 2017, Ted launched the *Capital Allocators* podcast, a series of interviews with leading Chief Investment Officers. The show reached four million downloads in August 2020. *Barron's*, *Business Insider*, *ValueWalk*, and *Forbes* each named it among the top investing podcasts. He also advises asset managers and allocators across business strategy, audio content, and investing.

Ted writes opinion pieces for *Institutional Investor*, wrote a blog for the CFA Institute's Enterprising Investor and guest publications for the late Peter L. Bernstein's *Economics and Portfolio Strategy*.

You can hear Ted's story in his own words on *Capital Allocators* episodes 45 (It's Not About the Money), 34 (Deep Dive on Hedge Funds), and 5 (The Bet with Buffett).

Acknowledgments

My father lost his parents at a young age. His father passed away at age 52, and my dad never thought he would live a day past that. Still smiling at 87, every day of the last 35 years has offered unexpected upside.

The *Capital Allocators* podcast has been the same for me. I started it without an objective or goal. Thanks to incredible guests, engaged listeners, the magic of compounding and optionality, the experience has offered a cornucopia of upside surprises.

The guests who share their stories are the stars of the show and receive my deepest gratitude. Almost all the guests who appeared during the first year are friends from my time in the business. Thank you for sharing our conversations publicly without any expectation of benefit. These talented professionals backed this endeavor with their time and wisdom and laid the groundwork for what happened since.

Guests repeatedly shared stories of tangible and intangible benefits that accrued to them after coming on the show. Most hear from old friends and colleagues, and many find it productive for their investing and business. It's been gratifying to deliver that goodwill and offer all future guests a hint that positive surprises will come out of their appearance. As a bonus, for every handful of guests who I didn't know before the podcast conversation, one has evolved into a meaningful relationship. I'm so glad we met in this way.

This show has created a virtual community. The audience is just as important as the guests to its strength. An engaged audience attracts great guests, which in turn helps keep the quality of content high and the audience growing. Our community of listeners ranges from leading allocators and money managers around the world to interested students of investing from all walks of life. Thank you for choosing to spend your precious time listening to the show.

Over the last three years, I've received countless notes of thanks. Each one reminds me that this effort is a lot bigger than me and energizes me to carry on. Thank you for those kind words.

Although I didn't set out to pursue this adventure as a livelihood, a series of serendipitous circumstances led to that outcome. I am deeply appreciative to all the advertisers, corporate sponsors, premium content members, and advisory clients who support the business around the show.

Patrick O'Shaughnessy has been my brother-in-arms on this journey. He has been my sounding board and thought partner on style, best practices, and the business of podcasting. He is a force of nature, an inspiration, and a wonderful friend.

Christopher Seifel is the catalyst who made this book happen. A year ago I reached out to my mailing list (www.capitalallocators.com) to ask for assistance in gleaning the best quotes from each show. Christopher went above and beyond, outlining each episode with a page and a half of quotes. I had thought about this project for a while but couldn't imagine finding the time to go back and review thousands of pages of transcripts. Part 3 of the book draws heavily on Christopher's outstanding curation of the episodes.

Connor Aller joined me as an intern two years ago to manage the behind the scenes production of the website and special projects. He has enthusiastically cranked through everything I asked of him, while performing at the highest level in his day job. Thanks Connor, I could not have had the bandwidth to take on this project without your help.

Craig Pearce at Harriman House approached me two years ago offering to publish any book I might consider writing in the future. He offered an economic partnership and delivered as a true partner in this project every step of the way. Thank you for your outstanding comments and suggestions that significantly improved the quality of this book.

Brian Portnoy and Erez Kalir are great friends and accomplished thinkers who graciously commented on a draft of this book and made it better than it could have been without their keen eyes. I am grateful for your assistance and friendship.

My wife Vanessa Schenck-Seides has been the wind beneath my wings since the day we met. Neither of us imagined that life would bring us together as it has, and I am incredibly grateful that it did. Thank you, my love, for encouraging me and laughing with me every step along the way.

I come from a family of teachers. My mother retired from running a preschool some time ago, and my sister works with special education students. My father taught graduate school alongside his medical practice for years, and my brother almost left his career in wireless telecom to teach business school. I always assumed I would find myself in a classroom. Apparently, I already have. Thank you for attending class each week and for picking up this textbook.

About *Capital Allocators*

Who are these capital allocators and why have conversations with them on the *Capital Allocators* podcast been listened to four million times?

Capital allocation is the process of deciding where to invest limited resources. It occurs when corporate executives decide how to fund operations and initiatives. It occurs when portfolio managers at investment firms select and size positions. And it occurs when Chief Investment Officers (CIOs) for end owners of capital commit to investment products. The concept of capital allocation pervades finance and its real-world consequences are far reaching.

I created the *Capital Allocators* podcast in 2017 to focus on this last group, the people who sit at the top of the global food chain of capital. When I refer to "allocators" in this book, it is the CIOs and their teams that I have in mind.

At the bottom of the food chain, businesses are conceived by entrepreneurs. They raise capital to pursue their ideas by selling a piece of their business or borrowing money with the intent to pay it back. They make business decisions about which products or services to create, markets to enter, and forms of financing to fund new projects or return capital. These decisions are important ones in the success of their business. They are also different from the decisions faced by CIOs.

The middle of the food chain is populated by money managers. When overseeing their business, they make choices like those of business executives. When producing their product, they make capital allocation decisions like CIOs, picking investments and constructing portfolios.

CIOs sit at the top of the food chain. Endowments and foundations, high net worth individuals, family offices, corporate and public pension funds, and sovereign wealth funds are end owners of capital. CIOs lead their investment operations.

End owners of capital frequently staff their investment team with a small number of professionals. The team occasionally invests directly in securities or deals, and more frequently allocates capital to the products run by money managers.

Money managers often specialize in one style of investing. For example, Andreessen Horowitz, or a16z (Scott Kupor – *Capital Allocators*, First Meeting episode 7), is a leading venture capital firm and Wellington Management (Jean Hynes – episode 82) is best known for public equity and fixed income management. Others are intermediaries, like Outsourced Chief Investment Officer (OCIO) Hirtle Callaghan (Jon Hirtle – episode 98), who raise capital from end owners and invest it in money management products.

There are so many specialized, well-resourced money managers in different strategies around the world that one sensible investment approach for CIOs is to identify the best of them across each area of expertise. CIOs partner with specialists, rather than hire a team to compete with them.

CIOs are students of the entire investment universe. They have a unique vantage point to look across assets, strategies, and geographies and build a portfolio of investments that best meets their objectives. They assess both the merits of the money management organization and the attractiveness of the underlying assets held by the manager. They have access and exposure to talented minds across the investment universe. Their seat is the broadest and most fascinating in all of investing, and their decisions significantly influence how capital flows throughout the world.

I started my career working for the most famous CIO in the world, David Swensen, who for 35 years has overseen the Yale University Investments Office. He is a brilliant investor and gifted teacher. A dozen of David's protégés manage some of the largest endowments and foundations.[*]

---

[*] My colleagues at Yale included Andy Golden, CIO of PRINCO, Ellen Shuman, former CIO of Carnegie Corp, Donna Dean, former CIO of Rockefeller Foundation, Mary McLean, former CIO of Kauffman Foundation, Seth Alexander, CIO of MITIMCo, Lauren Meserve, CIO of Metropolitan Museum of Art, Paula Volent, CIO of Bowdoin College, and Casey Whalen, CIO of Truvvo Partners. Other notable alumni who came after my time include Robert Wallace, CEO of Stanford Management Company, Kim Sargent, CIO of Packard Foundation, Peter Ammon, CIO of University of Pennsylvania, Anne Martin, CIO of Wesleyan University and Randy Kim, CIO of Rainwater Charitable Foundation.

In the 20 years after my apprenticeship at Yale, I continued to study money managers across public and private markets. Three and a half years ago, I created a podcast called *Capital Allocators* to share conversations with a range of CIOs around the world. I hoped to learn about different frameworks and best practices for how these holders of the keys to the kingdom allocate their time and money.

I never expected to write another book. Most first-time authors lose the naïve boon of seeing their name on a book jacket once they meet the reality that writing a book sucks up time and money, two of the most precious resources we have. Yet, here I am, sitting in front of my computer, following the serendipity that called me to put pen to paper once more.

After so many interviews with allocators, managers, and thought leaders – where each had wisdom to share about how to enhance the investment process – I no longer could retain all the information in my head. David Swensen's book remains the seminal tome in explaining the structure of capital allocation of institutional portfolios. This book is different. It endeavors to explain how these investors implement their craft.

My intent in writing is to help investors make better decisions. Investment success is increasingly challenging with every passing year, and the breadth of skills required to succeed expands commensurately. The lessons imparted by guests on the podcast speak to the needed skills and prerequisites for success going forward.

How to Use This Book

Capital Allocators is a distillation of lessons shared by guests on the first 150 episodes of the *Capital Allocators* podcast. It is presented in three distinct parts, each of which can best be digested in its own way.

The introduction tells the story of how the podcast came about and shares my thoughts on the active/passive debate. If you wholeheartedly believe that passive investing is the way to go, my apologies for having increased your investment spending by a few bucks. This book is intended for the rest of us.

Part 1 of the book is a toolkit. The chapters cover five necessary functional tools employed by allocators: interviewing, decision-making, negotiations, leadership, and management. Each of these chapters covers a distinct skill and can be read on its own. The flow of chapters follows a logical sequence, but you won't miss a beat hopping to the chapter that catches your eye.

Part 2 turns to the craft of investing. It is a set of investment frameworks summarizing how modern allocators think about and conduct the investment process. The chapters discuss governance, investment strategy, investment process, technological innovation, and a case study on dealing with uncertainty. The structure follows the thought process of CIOs from the 10,000-foot level down. I wrote it to be read sequentially, although you certainly can take a lot away from each chapter read individually if you choose.

Parts 1 and 2 just scratch the surface on these tools and frameworks of investing. The end of each chapter contains recommendations for podcasts, online resources, and books to take the next step in the learning process. Appendix B repeats these recommendations in one place.

Throughout these sections, ideas and quotes from guests on the show add color to the concepts. By convention, I have included the place of work for each guest the first time they are mentioned in the body of the text. Appendix C contains a full directory of guests, including their title or role.

Part 3 is full of quotes from the guests themselves. The research for writing this book entailed whittling 3,500 pages of transcripts down to a few hundred quotes. Many of those ideas shaped the toolkit and investment framework sections. One hundred and eighty-four of the remaining nuggets of wisdom are presented in this section. Read them as you see fit – straight through, one at a time, by topic, or whenever you seek some inspiration. The last chapter is a top 10 list of the best quotes from 150 hours of conversations.

Capital Allocators: How the world's elite money managers lead and invest is the reference manual for investing that I want to have on my desk.

I hope you find it the same.

Introduction

"Did you find the podcast, or did the podcast find you?"

– *Michael Mervosh*

On a wintry day in February 2016, I sat on a chairlift at Haystack Mountain in Vermont with my friend Gregg Clark. Gregg is a warm-hearted guy who I'm quite sure could be a world champion on *Jeopardy*. He holds encyclopedic knowledge of both the useful and useless, equally facile in the arcane details of financial models and the wisdom of the Toltec culture. An engineer by training, Gregg saw one weekend that the full-sized electronic bowling alley in the ski lodge had stopped working. He heard the manufacturer couldn't repair it until Monday, so he took the manual overnight and fixed it himself the next morning.

As we rode our way up the mountain, Gregg asked if I listened to podcasts. At the time, I had barely heard of a podcast and didn't know the purple app on my iPhone existed. He directed me to *The Tim Ferriss Show*, and I was hooked.

Around the same time, my first book *So You Want to Start a Hedge Fund: Lessons for Managers and Allocators* released. After 14 years focused on sourcing, researching, and investing in early-stage hedge funds, I had acquired a body of knowledge about the ecosystem that few aspiring entrepreneurs in the industry understood. I noticed I was having the same conversation repeatedly and decided to put pen to paper so more people could learn from the past lessons of others.

The book also marked the end of a chapter in my professional life. I was keen to leave a narrowly siloed world of investing in small hedge funds and get back to a broader mandate akin to where I started my career.

In this window of transition, I received invitations to share the lessons of the book publicly. I appeared on television, radio, and lo and behold, a series of podcasts. One podcast conversation stood out. In October 2016, I sat down to speak to Patrick O'Shaughnessy in what became the seventh episode of his podcast, *Invest Like the Best*. I was blown away by his preparation and ability to ask just the right questions. We became fast friends.

The experience with Patrick demystified what happens behind the curtain of podcasting. We met in his office and had a conversation in front of two microphones. It seemed as simple as that.

A short time afterwards, I saw a Facebook post that my college friend Chris Douvos was a guest on a different podcast. Chris is the highly entertaining 'Super LP' of venture capital and founder of Ahoy Capital. I listened and was appalled. The questioning was so rote and scripted and the energy so low that the hosts managed to make Chris sound dull. If you listen to my conversation with Chris (*Capital Allocators*, Ep.14), you'll understand that it's quite a feat to crush his energy.

That day, a lightbulb went off in my head. I had time on my hands and wanted to reconnect with some of my old friends who I didn't have time to see in the day-to-day grind of managing money. I aspired to interview with Patrick's natural dexterity, and I figured I could do better than the folks who interviewed Chris.

I created a podcast interviewing people who are tasked with managing large pools of capital. I called Patrick to inquire about how it all worked. He sent me on a voyage to purchase a laundry list of equipment, record a few conversations, and connect with Mathew Passy to assist with the production. Off I went.

I recorded a fantastic conversation with my friend Steve Galbraith, who had written the foreword for *So You Want to Start a Hedge Fund*. I guided the conversation through Steve's remarkable career and filtered in fun stories about his owning a local brewery and European football team. I couldn't believe how well the conversation went and was excited to share it.

There was only one problem. I lost the recording.

For the next six hours I couldn't find the recording on my H6 Handy Recorder. I searched the internet for a solution, called customer service at the manufacturer, and reached out to Mathew. All of it was to no avail. I was about to declare the end of my nascent podcasting venture when I thought of calling Gregg Clark, the one person who might have an answer when no one else did. Sure enough, Gregg hooked up the device to his computer, plugged in a few extra wires, hit play, and an hour and 11 minutes later downloaded a perfect digital recording of the episode out of thin air.

Before launching the podcast, I recorded two more conversations with dear friends. One was with André Perold, my former business school professor. The other was with Paula Volent, my former colleague and star endowment manager at Bowdoin College. A week later Paula called to inform me that she couldn't get permission to put it on air. My plan to launch with three episodes got cut by one-third just like that.

I released the episodes with Steve and André and sent an email to friends in my contacts. Two hundred of them listened to one of the initial episodes. From there, I asked some friends to join me for an interview. A few conversations turned into a few more and three and a half years later, here we are.

* * *

That's the chronological story of how the podcast came together, but there's another side to the story that is harder to explain. Michael Mervosh described a different way of moving through the world during our podcast conversation. He posed the question, "Did I find the podcast, or did the podcast find me?"

The podcast journey was one of the first times in my life that I took on a professional challenge without a goal in mind. I thought it would be a fun and productive way to spend some time while searching for my next full-time engagement. If nothing else, I suspected the adventure would create some optionality, even if I had no idea what those options might be.

I was full of doubts when getting started. The only thing I knew for sure was that I didn't like the sound of my own voice and was fairly confident others wouldn't either. I didn't know if I would interview well or if I would be able to keep a conversation flowing. I wondered if I would run out of guests to interview, of subjects to discuss, or of time to keep going. And I never once thought of the podcast as a business, as even a cursory level of analysis would have suggested that offering content for free to a finite natural audience is not a road to riches. But I really didn't care about that, because I was ready to try something new without feeling tied to an outcome.

As a result, I can't explain what happened over the last three and a half years. I sent out one email, started posting episodes on my empty LinkedIn and Twitter accounts, and through word-of-mouth the 200 downloads that first week grew to 20,000× that number in a trajectory that looks like a stock chart presented in thousands of manager pitchbooks.

WEEKLY DOWNLOADS OF *CAPITAL ALLOCATORS*[1]

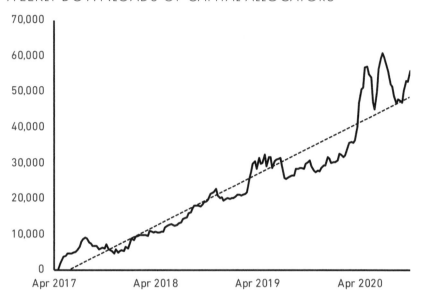

I started receiving positive feedback from old friends and new. Some commented on my excellent "voice for radio," rebuffing the only definitive prior I held. Others reflected an interview style of humility and curiosity that I would describe as a mirror of my best self. Most importantly, the podcast guests universally derived value from the experience, commenting on the platitudes and unexpected benefits they received after coming on the show. I loved being in the business of building goodwill.

As I released episodes one week after the next, I started to realize I had come across an educational platform unlike anything else available. I had the privilege of working with many top-flight investors in my two decades of experience, and 45 of the first 50 podcast guests were friends and peers from that time.

I hadn't quite appreciated how little these insightful investors were in the public eye. One of my favorite examples came from Jim Williams, the long-time CIO of the Getty Trust. Following our conversation, Jim mentioned how much he had learned from the podcast with his peer, Scott Malpass, the recently retired CIO of Notre Dame University. I was surprised, knowing that the two had been friends for decades. Jim explained that although they speak a few times a year, he never before had the chance to hear Scott's story in its entirety. At that moment, I realized that I hadn't either, nor had just about anyone else.

My guiding light in building the roster of guests has been answering the questions of who I am curious to speak to now, and what I would like to learn. I love hearing personal stories – investing is indeed a people business – so all the episodes start that way. Many guests fit into my original concept of diving into the people, philosophy, and process of the holders of the keys to the kingdom in asset management. I've also explored other disciplines that help allocators of capital think about improving their skill set.

Three years into this adventure, the podcast has gone beyond my expectations and been great fun. I've had wonderful conversations with brilliant thinkers and met incredible people along the way. It has proven a fruitful exercise in what Patrick has dubbed "growth without goals."

Before we get to the lessons from the many guests on the show, I want to share some thoughts about the active vs. passive debate. The podcast and this book are entirely about the pursuit of active management through allocation to money managers. Critics of active management think this entire pursuit is a folly. I disagree, so let me tell you why.

Active versus Passive

"Only a fool would enter lightly into a wager against the Oracle of Omaha, especially when he has put his judgment about an important investment matter to the test."[2]

– *Ted Seides (yes, that was me)*

The case for passive management

Capital markets finished 2019 with a decade of exceedingly strong returns. A simple, traditional 60% stock/40% bond portfolio in the United States generated 11% per annum for the decade, far surpassing the 7–8% annual spending needs of most institutions.

Active managers by and large underperformed the indexes during this period, with 87% of active U.S. equity managers falling short of the returns of the S&P 500.[3] This single, often cited statistic simplifies a more nuanced comparison, which could include active strategies across geographies, capitalization, style, and capital structure. But the point is clear. The decade did not shine brightly on the asset management industry.

If there was a winner in the mix, it was The Vanguard Group. The king of passive management and one of three firms comprising the lion's share of index products,* Vanguard became synonymous with its low-cost investing philosophy. The organization grew from $1 trillion[4] to $6.2 trillion in assets under management since the onset of the financial crisis.[5]

I was at the forefront of the active-passive debate in a public setting. In 2007 I initiated a ten-year bet with Warren Buffett that pitted Vanguard's

---

* Alongside Blackrock and State Street.

S&P 500 index fund against a portfolio of high-cost hedge funds, represented by the selection of five hedge fund-of-fund products. Carol Loomis chronicled the initiation of the bet in a *Fortune* magazine article.[6] At the time, my partners and I assessed our chances of winning at 85%; Warren put his odds at 60%.

I wrote a white paper describing my rationale for making the wager at the time.[7] Stocks appeared priced at historically rich valuations in 2007, and hedge funds seemed a good alternative to help institutional investors meet spending needs. The comparison of a stock market to a portfolio of hedge funds is like comparing apples to oranges, owing in part to different market exposures, risk, and tax treatment. Nevertheless, it seemed a good bet to make at the time.

Suffice it to say, the bet did not turn out well for the hedge fund side of the ledger. It launched on January 1, 2008 and only 14 months later, the hedge funds held a lead of approximately 50%. Once the Fed backstopped the market in March 2009, there may not have been another quarter in the subsequent 8¾ years in which hedge funds outperformed the soaring S&P.

If identical circumstances to those in 2007 presented today, I would still make the bet. I reviewed my decision-making process employing some of the tools described in Chapter 2, Decision-Making, and spoke to Warren about his process at the time. I believe the decision to bet on hedge funds was a good one.

Some of the smartest people I know in the business don't agree. Charley Ellis, the venerable founder of Greenwich Associates and author of 16 books on investing, first wrote about the power of indexing in 1985 in his seminal tome, *Investment Policy: Winning the Loser's Game.*[8] He argued 35 years ago that so many smart, hard-working active investors were flooding the market that together they would offset each other. As a result, owning the market through an index fund was a better strategy.

In 2016, Charley published *The Index Revolution: Why Investors Should Join It Now.* Thirty-one years after his initial description, he presented a series of compelling facts describing the same phenomenon. The surge in CFA Charterholders, the ubiquity of data, and the speed at which information is disseminated has created what Michael Mauboussin of Counterpoint Global refers to as the paradox of skill. Yes, the absolute skill of investors is higher than it has ever been, but the breadth of that skill across so many outstanding participants has narrowed the relative skill against each other. It is harder to outperform the market than it has ever been.

Passive management proponents all point out that investing in the public markets is a zero-sum game. For every investor who wins, another must lose. In aggregate, active managers earn the market return and charge a fee along the way, turning the zero sum game into a negative sum game.

The case for active management

The case for passive management is nearly bulletproof in theory. It is also nearly irrelevant in the practice of institutional asset management today. From here onwards, a simple 60/40 portfolio of U.S. stocks and bonds is unlikely to generate sufficient returns to meet spending needs. Stepping outside of that passive portfolio requires skill to succeed.

After the surge in stocks and bonds for a decade, capital market pricing leaves little juice to squeeze out of the lemon. Consider the following metrics as of October 31, 2020: The 10-Year US Treasury yields 0.9%, dividend yield on the S&P 500 is 2%, and the projected long-term growth rate of earnings of the S&P 500 is 6%. Holding future valuation multiples constant, a rough estimate of the long-term nominal expected returns of a 60/40 portfolio in the U.S. is a touch below 5% per annum.

Money manager GMO believes high valuation multiples will not remain constant and the outlook is much worse. Its seven-year asset class forecast incorporates expectations for a reversion to the mean to lower market multiples and profit margins. The same 60/40 mix in GMO's projections results in a −4% annual real return as of October 31, 2020, or approximately a −2% nominal return at breakeven inflation rates.

When an institution looks out over the next decade, they will find that a 60/40 portfolio of U.S. stocks and bonds won't do the trick. Endowments and foundations typically target 5% real returns (6–7% nominal). Pension funds have 7–8% actuarial rates of return. Any reasonable projections of a passive 60/40 stock-bond portfolio won't keep up with spending needs.

Further, the implementation of an investment strategy beyond a traditional 60/40 mix requires active decisions. A CIO must consider which markets to own, which indexes to employ, and in what proportions. Charley Ellis himself discussed these challenges in our two podcast conversations.

While staunchly supporting index fund management, Charley noted that active management is preferable in emerging markets and probably in Europe too. Selecting active managers is also required to participate in private equity and venture capital. Charley is passionate about the index fund movement, but he is equally passionate about the unusual success of Capital Group, Yale University, and Vanguard – that is, the little-known team at Vanguard that selects active managers, not the indexing juggernaut itself.

Lastly, passive management is a rounding error when considering how the most successful allocators in the world apply their trade. The Yale University endowment is one example. Only 10% of Yale's policy portfolio is allocated to U.S. stocks, bonds and cash, and only approximately 14% more is invested in international equities. The remaining 76% of Yale's portfolio is invested in assets that have no readily accessible index fund to earn low-cost, easy-to-access returns.

Yale is playing a completely different game than that easily available to individuals, and so are the other CIOs around the world who have appeared on *Capital Allocators*. The staunch proponents of index fund management might want to consider why some of the smartest people in the business have independently chosen to pursue strategies that cannot be indexed. Perhaps the wisdom of this crowd is entirely wrong and investment success is easy, but I doubt it.

Albert Einstein once said, "Everything should be made as simple as possible, but no simpler." I believe the active/passive debate is full of nuance that is lost in proclaiming the failure of active management. Both active and passive are valuable tools that can serve important purposes in achieving investment success.

Active management success is far from a foregone conclusion. It requires atypical skill from managers, a keen eye and an extensive professional network to spot those skills from an allocator, and a lot of work by both to stay ahead of the crowd. It requires a set of learned tools, skill sets, and insights beyond anything available in academic literature.

This book is decidedly about the active management process – how the holders of the keys to the kingdom allocate their time and their capital to meet the needs of their institutions. Make no bones about it: investment success going forward will require making outstanding decisions about asset allocation, manager selection, and security selection. Passive investing is poorly positioned to meet spending needs, and active management is increasingly competitive. We need to take this craft as seriously as ever. Attempting to do so without the requisite skill set at your disposal is a recipe for underperformance.

If you agree, let's turn to the set of tools that capital allocators need to maximize their chance of success.

1

TOOLKIT

When I joined private equity firm Stonebridge Partners after business school, Bob Raziano was the lead operating partner at the firm. Bob had been one of the youngest partners at consulting firm Booz Allen and rose to the role of Chief Financial and Administrative Officer at CS First Boston before joining Stonebridge. I remember visiting a manufacturer of metallized paper with him and marvelling at his ability to systematically break down every aspect of the business during due diligence. I asked if he used a checklist. He responded that his apprenticeship in management consulting early in his career was like being handed a ruler to measure how to dissect companies.

Similarly, CIOs need a set of tools to break down the complex task of managing large pools of capital. Talented CIOs are skilled at both listening carefully and speaking in public, both learning and educating, both thinking independently and orchestrating a group, both managing a team and a governance board, and each of reading, writing and arithmetic. The best ones are the equivalent of Major League Baseball's five-tool players.

Acquiring such a broad set of skills draws on many different disciplines. The interviews on the podcast with CIOs, investment managers, and thought leaders from outside of the investment industry collectively teach best practices around each of these skills.

These lessons are not found in the readings in the CFA program, CAIA curriculum, or other investment materials. Just as my first book, *So You Want to Start a Hedge Fund*, shares case studies about start-up hedge funds from the front lines, this section describes skill sets that are only encountered in practice. Importantly, these chapters do not present definitive research on the topics. They are a compilation of lessons gleaned from my experiences and those of guests on the show.

The toolkit in Part 1 explores the major disciplines required of CIOs:

- Interviewing
- Decision-making
- Negotiations
- Leadership
- Management

We'll start with interviewing, a practice that allocators engage in just about every day.

Chapter 1
Interviewing

"I've learned that people will forget what you said, people will forget what you did, but people will never forget how you made them feel."

— Maya Angelou

The core interaction in the investment process is a series of interviews. Across 20 years in the business, I conducted interviews with money managers two or three times a day, totaling thousands. In all that time, I only peripherally thought about the process of interviewing until I started the podcast.

The lessons I learned by studying professional interviewers and conducting podcasts over the last three years follow this process:

- Defining the purpose
- Preparing
- Setting the stage
- Listening actively
- Receiving feedback
- Additional interviewing tips

In the investment world, these lessons are applicable to manager interviews and reference checking.

Defining the purpose

Interviews are different from conversations. Conversations are casual discussions between people. They are back and forth interactions often balanced in airtime.

Interviews are conversations with a purpose. For the most part, interviewers ask the questions and interviewees answer. An allocator's purpose in a manager interview is to gather information and evaluate the manager on both content and persona. CIOs seek to confirm or refute the validity of their hypothesis for investing in the manager. At the same time, each interview offers an opportunity to learn about social interactions and trustworthiness for a partnership that may last years or decades. These interviews require focus and attention in every aspect of the conversation.

That purpose sounds straightforward, but we've all experienced ineffective meetings in which the objective gets subjugated to an allocator peacocking by expressing their views to prove their intellectual worth. Tom Bushey found in his initial market meetings for Sunderland Capital that probably two-thirds of the people interviewing him told him why what he was doing was ludicrous and how they would do it instead.

A podcast interview is different. I discuss many of the same subjects I did when interviewing as an allocator, but evaluation is no longer my objective. I let CIOs and investment managers tell their stories, and I have no need to decide if I want to invest with them afterwards.

Other forms of interviewing carry a different purpose and call on different skills. Jon Wertheim has written and conducted interviews for *Sports Illustrated* and *60 Minutes* for 25 years. His interviews have sought quotes for stories, entertainment for television, and facts for journalistic investigations. When filling a story with a quote, Jon wants just one nugget. A half-hour conversation can be horrible for 29 minutes, but if the subject gives a sound bite when wrapping up, he will have accomplished his mission. He may purposefully express boredom, excitement or provocation, all in the interest of getting one little gem.

His television interviews are the opposite. The medium requires a cadence and flow throughout that matters as much as the material. If the interviewer and subject interrupt each other, the television viewing will be poor and will usurp otherwise great content.

Investigative journalism is different again. Conducting research for a story requires in-depth probing and verbal interrogation techniques where substance matters more than style.

The style and techniques of interviewing across podcasts, stories, television, and investigations are all different from the evaluative interviews conducted by allocators. At the same time, the different disciplines share common techniques that are effective across the board and useful for allocators to improve their skills for evaluating managers.

Preparing

Sitting in-between managers and clients as the co-CIO of a fund of funds, I was stunned how frequently interviews took place with no prior preparation. Time in front of managers is limited. Wasting that time drawing out easily accessible information that could have been learned in advance is highly inefficient.

Great interactions come from preparing to blend structure and flow in the conversation. Interviewing legends Larry King and Cal Fussman take different approaches that both rely on detailed preparation. Larry conducts research and develops an outline for the interview. He never contemplates specific questions ahead of time.[9] Cal does his research by creating a long list of interview questions, picking out a few of his favorites, reading them carefully, and then throwing away the list before he conducts the actual interview. He plans for the conversation without getting anchored to specific questions.[10]

I had the opportunity to vary my degree of preparation across podcast interviews. In the first few podcasts, I massively overprepared. I created long question lists and brought them into the session with me. In the actual interview, the question list was a weighty anchor. I glimpsed at it often to make sure I didn't miss anything, distracted myself, and whiffed on asking obvious follow-up questions as a result. That over-preparation created a rigid agenda that took me away from being present and in the flow of the conversation.

The more I backed off prepared questions, the more I trusted my instincts to follow up with questions in a dialogue. At one point, I grew sufficiently comfortable that I toyed around with skipping my preparation entirely.

I underprepared and got by, but I knew the interview would have been better if I had put in the work. I ultimately found a sweet spot in preparing outlines for the flow of conversation and steering clear of specifics, blending a structure with open space to allow the conversation to flow naturally.

Allocators can similarly do homework in advance of a meeting to discover areas of exploration. This preparation includes reading all available materials and past meeting notes, determining an objective for the meeting, and structuring the meeting to elicit information. In Appendix A, I share a sample outline and Cal Fussman-like set of questions to help prepare for a first meeting with a long-short equity hedge fund manager.

Meeting objectives may vary. Early meetings focus on information gathering and getting to know the principals. Meetings with long-standing managers in a portfolio may dive into a specific investment, theme or organizational issue. Each meeting may call for a different set of questions, depending on the investment strategy, team, process, and risk appropriate to implement that strategy.

Allocators also consider the organization of the meeting itself – who is attending from both sides, who will lead the questioning, and how will they interpret verbal responses and body language. Conducting manager interviews with more than one person expands the team's bandwidth to divide and conquer, with one focusing on questions and content and another on behavior and style.

Setting the stage

Manager interviews are designed to gather information, so talented allocators can create an environment to elicit as much information as possible. People open up when they are at ease. The physical setting of the interview can be an important factor in the tone of the discussion.

Most manager meetings take place across the table in a conference room, a directly confrontational set-up. Over time, allocators find ways to spend time with managers away from that setting. Scott Malpass regularly invited managers to attend Notre Dame football games. Jon Harris of Alternative Investment Management goes out to dinner with a manager and their spouse or significant other in advance of allocating capital. CIOs exercise, play sports, and attend cultural or charity events with managers to learn more about their personality. I once backed away from an investment after playing golf with a manager and observing how abysmally he treated the caddie. The outing helped explain why his organization had experienced an unsettling amount of personnel turnover.

Beyond the physical setting, an allocator's tone and style in the interview can also influence the manager's degree of openness. Allocators can consider a number of shared lessons that help foster a productive chemistry in manager meetings.

1. Find common ground

We are inclined to embrace those who are like us. Discovering commonality across backgrounds, relationships, or interests at the onset of a meeting can go a long way towards shifting the tone of the interview from transactional to relationship-oriented.

2. Ask simple, brief questions

Jon Wertheim discovered that simple and brief questions are the most effective across all formats. He noted:

> It's taken me way too long to learn that sometimes less is more, and a simple question and letting the subject fill in any silence is better than jumping in and trying to prove that you belong at the table.

He further suggests avoiding a common temptation to show how much research you've done and how smart you are. Remembering that at the end of the day, it's about a connection.

3. Start with how, what, or why?

Open-ended questions that start with How, What, or Why provide space for managers to tell their story. By phrasing questions in a way that encourages broad answers, allocators can glean information beyond the particulars of the question they had in mind.

4. Let people talk

My uncle used to say, "You have two ears and one mouth, so listen twice as much as you speak." It is amazing what you can learn when you let people talk. If the purpose of conducting an interview is to learn, then it should follow that allocators listen far more than they speak.

5. Express humility

Investing is a humbling business, even for the best managers. Allocators can similarly be humble. The best interviewers are not afraid to ask naive questions. Asking for help to better understand the basics is a welcoming approach.

6. Be curious

An allocator's job offers the gift of continuous learning. Approaching interviews from an inquisitive perspective rather than an evaluative one allows allocators to take in all the information available from a manager. Tom Russo at Gardner Russo & Gardner has a knack for remembering details of his conversations. When he hears something surprising, he regularly follows up with personal notes recalling those facts.

7. Lose the script

The best interviews flow unpredictably. Thorough preparation includes an outline and list of questions, but sticking too closely to a prescribed Q&A will create distractions from hearing what the manager is saying and asking clever follow-up questions.

Active listening

Once the preparation is complete and the meeting begins, great interviewers become great listeners. Charley Ellis describes the importance of listening to the success of Capital Group:

> John Lovelace had a very strong interest in helping people learn how to be very good at listening. Not listening to hear what was said, but listening to hear what was meant and what was

different from last time. That's very helpful when you're trying to learn about companies, but it's also great when you're working with the other folks preparing to make a decision for the fund.[11]

Listening to learn is at the heart of a successful interview. It entails clearing your mind of distractions, being present, and paying attention to what the subject is saying without reacting. Listening gets blocked when thoughts pop into your head, and you can't let them go. The set of tools to listen actively in an interview include noting distractions, mirroring, validating, and empathising.

1. Noting distractions

Listening without cluttering your mind with thoughts is challenging. Like a meditation practice, noting when your mind drifts and bringing it back to the conversation keeps an interviewer focused on the content at hand.

2. Mirroring

I first got exposed to mirroring at a relationship workshop taught by Harville Hendrix nearly 20 years ago. Since then, I found the same concept as a core tenet of communication across casual conversation, spousal relationships, business decision-making, and hostage negotiation. Interviewing managers is another use case for mirroring.

Mirroring is parroting back what someone says, although it sounds a lot simpler than it is in practice. Good follow-up questions often arise spontaneously from something an interview subject has just said. By repeating back parts of their thoughts, you can ensure you have listened and let them know they have been heard. Mirroring leverages neural resonance, slows down the pace of conversation, and softens emotional triggers. As a result, it creates a magically safe space to communicate.

3. Validating

Validation is the process of letting the other person know that what they said is logical. Whether or not you agree with the points made, you can confirm that they have followed a sensible thought process.

Effective validation requires presence. Oftentimes, we have a different opinion about what the interviewee is saying and react. The trick in validating is confirming their perspective without needing to agree with it.

4. Empathizing

Expressing emotional empathy can open up an interviewee to discuss difficult subjects. Empathy is often the antithesis of what investors expect to encounter in the world of money, as it moves away from thoughts and touches on feelings.

Receiving feedback

Most investment professionals are not frequent solicitors of feedback, in stark contrast to participants in most high-performance fields. Elite athletes have coaches and business executives have boards and reviews, but investment managers carry on independently in their own bubble.

Among the podcast interviews I have conducted, only two guests went out of their way to explicitly request feedback on their performance. Who are those two you ask? Author and former poker champion Annie Duke and Farnam Street creator Shane Parrish – two experts in human behavior and decision-making. Having studied the field, they know the importance of receiving feedback.

Conducting post-mortems on interviews can be a valuable tool for both podcasting and investing. Podcasts are recorded interviews, which gives me the opportunity to listen back and critique my work afterwards. I regularly listen to my interviews to spot my ever-changing flaws, and periodically ask others to do the same. I frequently unearth different inflections in the sound of my voice, missed questions, and verbal tics. I figured out that asking a compound question usually results in the guest only answering the second part of the question, and that shortening questions prevents me from influencing the guest's answer. Similarly, allocators can debrief about manager interviews with team members to critique their performance.

Additional tips

Some of the most effective interviewing techniques come from one-off tips. The five whys, favorite questions of guests, and the application of interviewing tools to conducting reference checks are among the most useful in a CIO's arsenal.

1. The five whys

For decades, Japanese manufacturers were the best in the world, and Toyota was renowned for its Production System. I read a case study in business school on Toyota that included a discussion of the "Five Whys." To get to the root of a problem, the manager on a production line asked questions starting with the word "why" five times. Taiichi Ohno, the former Executive Vice President of Toyota Motor and pioneer of the Toyota Production System in the 1950s, offers this example.[12]

1. Why did the robot stop?

The circuit was overloaded, causing the fuse to blow.

2. Why was the circuit overloaded?

There was insufficient lubrication on the bearings, so they locked up.

3. Why was there insufficient lubrication on the bearings?

The oil pump on the robot was not circulating sufficient oil.

4. Why was the pump not circulating sufficient oil?

The pump intake was clogged with metal shavings.

5. Why was the intake clogged with metal shavings?

Because there was no filter on the pump.

Each question in Ohno's example mirrors a piece of the answer to a previous question. The Five Whys is rooted in the Japanese concept of *kaizen*, or continuous improvement.

2. Favorite questions

Allocators investigate the key drivers of a manager's success as they move along in the process. Some popular topics explore a manager's incentives, competitive advantage, self-awareness, culture, competitive landscape, and expectations. Allocators cleverly ask simple questions, hiding the in-depth thought process that qualifies the answers. Guests on the show have shared some of their favorite questions below. Those without attribution are some of mine.

a. Incentives

- "Are you still having fun?" – Adam Blitz
- "How do you invest your personal capital?"

Adam Blitz at Evanston Capital asks a generic question to assess continued motivation. He listens to detect the manager's passion for and engagement in the business and to hear what they choose to talk about.

Aligning incentives is the most important feature of an external manager relationship, and a manager's personal investment alongside clients is the most direct form of that alignment. Perspectives differ on the appropriate amount a manager should invest, however most agree that the amount should be substantial and serve to align risk tolerance. Doing so creates an "alignment of appetites" according to Andy Golden at Princeton University Investment Management Company. Probing about a manager's other personal investments can shed light on their risk tolerance and on other potentially attractive investment opportunities.

b. Competitive advantage

- "What is your superpower?" – Mario Therrien
- "What is your edge and why is it enduring?" – Bill Spitz
- "What is the compulsion that keeps you going?" – Patrick O'Shaughnessy
- "If you could brag about something exceptional without fear of appearing arrogant, what would that be?" – Jason Karp

Teasing out what makes a manager different and special can be difficult to ascertain by asking rote questions. Thoughtfully worded questions set the table for managers to reveal subtle differences in their approach and expertise.

c. Self-awareness

- "What's the best piece of feedback or criticism you've ever gotten from one of your partners and how did you apply those lessons?" – Chris Douvos
- "Do you have any questions for me?" – Doug Phillips
- "What would your former partners/analysts say about you?"

Great managers are self-aware and continuously improving. Questions that focus on where they are in their journey help allocators understand their mental dexterity. Doug Phillips at the University of Rochester Endowment throws out the seemingly innocuous question at the end of interviews as a test of a manager's innate inquisitiveness.

d. Process

- "Tell me about an idea that you did a ton of research on but did not ultimately make it into the portfolio?" – Brian Portnoy
- "Which position in your portfolio is least reflective of your investment style?" – Jason Klein
- "Tell me about a time when you failed epically." – Jenny Heller
- "What do you know now that you wish you knew 10 years ago?" – Mark Baumgartner
- "Every manager has been terminated. Which *three* of your clients most recently terminated your firm and why?" – Charley Ellis

Brian Portnoy, of Shaping Wealth, and Jason Klein, of Memorial Sloan Kettering Cancer Center, probe about specific situations that reveal the discipline and consistency in a manager's stated process. Jenny Heller, of Brandywine Group Advisors, and Mark Baumgartner, of the Institute for Advanced Study, both like to inquire about past mistakes. Jenny's inclusion of "epically" piques attention. Charley Ellis asks for three examples to get past the canned and easy response of just one and implicitly asks about their learning process at a time when it might be easy to pass up a teachable moment.

e. Team dynamics

- "What creates social capital in your organization?" – Kim Lew

- "What do you do for fun?" – Margaret Chen
- "How do you make decisions?" – Jim Williams
- "What types of interpersonal conflicts have arisen and how did you handle them?"

Teams are complex organisms. Learning about their formal interactions and informal norms helps allocators determine the likely stability and longevity of the enterprise.

Kim Lew, of Columbia Investment Management Company, dives into the culture of an organization by exploring social norms. She wants to figure out what gets rewarded in the organization. Sometimes working late hours is considered exemplary, other times it may be helping others, giving feedback, training analysts, or kissing up to the boss.

Margaret Chen of Cambridge Associates can catch managers off guard towards the end of an interview with a personal pop-up question that often is met with an unrehearsed answer. Her question is intended to understand what makes someone tick, how they lead, and how they experience the world. She finds that those who "live, eat, and breathe investments" are worrisome because of the bubble they form around that passion.

Jim Williams asks a simple question with the intent of following up with at least five "whys". His follow-ups probe about consistency across the team, degree of input, resolution of differences, hierarchy of the organization, safety and diversity of thought, and repeatability of the process. He seeks organizations in which everyone understands and supports the process.

f. Expectations

- "What are the circumstances when your strategy will perform poorly? How do you deal with those conditions?" – Seth Masters
- "If you fail to meet your expectations in five years, what will your post-mortem say?" – Jenny Heller
- "How do you define success?" – Tom Lenehan
- "What is the capacity of your strategy and what will you commit to do when you reach it?" – Dawn Fitzpatrick
- "How rough a drawdown would you consider normal for the strategy?"

An allocator can improve their quantitative assessment of a fund by comparing their expectation to that of the manager, ensuring they are on the same page.

g. Competitors

- "If you had to invest all your savings with one of your peers, who would it be and why? – Dawn Fitzpatrick
- "What do you do better than *(name specific competitor)*?"

Asking questions about the competitive landscape allows allocators to piece together a mosaic of opportunities and calibrate the relative merits of the manager they are considering.

3. Reference checks

Near the end of a due diligence process, allocators conduct exhaustive reference checks on managers. This final set of interviews has the intention of confirming beliefs about the people and process, fine-tuning expectations, and getting a relationship off to a flying start. Checks on public market managers tend to focus on character and expectations. Private market manager references also probe into the manager's impact on prior investment outcomes.

The set-up of reference checks creates a different and trickier dynamic than manager interviews. Reference checks are typically conducted over the phone with someone the allocator does not know and may not interact with again. Further, the referee is usually more beholden to the manager than the allocator. Each reference comes with their own bias and agenda, and allocators must take their expression of support with a grain of salt.

Thorough allocators call names on a reference list despite the likelihood of bias in favor of the manager. I found it surprising how infrequently references get called, particularly for popular managers where allocators may rely on the wisdom of crowds. Occasionally, on-list references share that they are not that enthusiastic about the manager. If the few chosen references are not wildly enthusiastic and that information comes without a rationale as to why, the allocator may want to take a step back and dig deeper.

The most important question an allocator asks of on-list references may be the one Kip McDaniel of *Institutional Investor* asks of every subject: "Who else should I talk to about this?" Getting off-list references can offer less biased perspectives about the manager and help uncover any potential issues.

Allocators can consider a full 360-degree perspective, inquiring about a manager's former bosses, peers, and subordinates. One favorite of mine was speaking to the manager's former administrative assistant.* The less-varnished the reference, the closer the allocator gets to objectivity. I once went as far as to call the ex-girlfriend of a prospective manager. I can't say she welcomed the call, but I can tell you her reflections about her ex served as the final confirmation for our investment thesis that led to a productive investment.

Reference check questions tend to attempt moves like ju-jitsu, positioning the subject to reveal information with natural momentum. Some good examples include the following:**

- Why are you serving as a reference?
- If he has a blind spot, what would it be? (Best asked as a follow-up from, "If he has a superpower, what would it be?")
- What would a naysayer say about him?
- Why might a former colleague say *x*? (where *x* is an area of concern)
- If you were in my shoes, what questions would you ask?
- What advice would you give them?
- Would you put your parents'/grandparents' money with her?

Summary

Over the last few years, I regularly re-engaged in my past work investing in managers and advising allocators. On one occasion, I caught up with an investment manager on behalf of a foundation for whom I serve

---

* This reference check worked best when my administrative assistant conducted the call.
** I found these examples from answers to a question I posted on Twitter. For this audience, Twitter can be a wonderful crowdsourced encyclopedia. Follow me @tseides and join in!

on the investment committee. Rather than assume my prior allocator evaluative interviewing style, I naturally began the meeting as I had grown accustomed to from the podcast. We connected personally, reviewed the investment program philosophically, and then talked strategy. I listened actively, mirrored, asked why, and explored topics of interest in the portfolio. To my pleasant surprise, the conversation was richer and revealed more about the manager than any I had conducted with him previously.

Investment teams interview managers every day. Preparation, setting the stage, listening, and feedback all contribute to interviewing skill.

Hours upon hours spent interviewing managers leave allocators with a wealth of information to make decisions about the managers to hire, retain, or replace. The process of making good decisions is tricky, so let's turn to that to make sure all these interviews don't go to waste.

To learn more

Podcasts

The Tim Ferriss Show: The Interview Master: Cal Fussman and the Power of Listening (Ep.145)

Invest Like the Best: The Ace of Spades, with Eric Maddox (Ep.15)

Books

Getting the Love You Want, Harville Hendrix

Chapter 2
Decision-Making

"If Danny Kahneman still commits these behavioral errors himself, how is Drew Dickson not going to?"

– Drew Dickson

Back in 2007, a good friend of mine led the due diligence on a European hedge fund run by a former Soros Fund Management portfolio manager. My friend was the head of research at a large fund of funds and was incredibly thorough. In fact, his team's work was so deep that managers referred to their process as a proctology exam.

My firm had seeded the hedge fund a few years before and after a strong stretch of performance, it crossed $1 billion in assets. I watched my friend and his team gather more information about the fund than anyone else. They understood everything about the manager and his approach and confirmed every detail along the way. I don't ever recall seeing more t-s crossed and i-s dotted.

During the process, he learned that the fund's returns were volatile. Historically, his firm preferred managers that delivered a smooth return stream. When we discussed the potential mismatch, he shared that his investment committee was looking to add more juice to their portfolio.

With all the information available in their hands, the investment committee approved a substantial investment. Sure enough, the fund hit a rough patch shortly thereafter and within a year, the fund of funds redeemed. I have wondered what happened that day in the committee meeting ever since.

* * *

All the information gleaned from interviewing and conducting due diligence on managers can go for naught if an allocator does not follow an effective decision-making process.

And here's the problem: we are hardwired to make poor decisions.

The field of behavioral economics sheds light on this unfortunate set of conditions. The human brain is designed to survive in the wild. Generations ago a fight or flight response was the difference between life and death. Daniel Kahneman referred to this instinct for action as System 1 thinking in his book, *Thinking, Fast and Slow*.[13] Most decisions we make are based on instinctive reactions. Occasionally, we consciously shift to System 2 thinking in which we carefully process information.

A CIO seeks to follow a sound process and get as close as possible to discovering the truth with the information available at the time. It follows the tagline of the Alliance for Decision Education, a non-profit co-founded by Annie Duke, "what is true and what to do."[14]

We'll start by developing an understanding of why it is so hard to make good decisions and then turn to how to improve the process.

Why this is so hard

Annie Duke, poker legend and author of *Thinking in Bets*[15] and *How to Decide*,[16] spent 20 years at a petri dish for decision-making: the poker table. In each hand of poker, she would make moves, obtain real-time feedback, and have an opportunity to assess her decision process.

Annie's research in the field helped her understand why people make bad decisions. Decisions are like bets that arise from beliefs about the way the world works. When a CIO buys a stock or a fund, they are betting on their belief that the investment is better than the many other options of putting the money to work.

The way humans form beliefs is counterintuitive. One might think that we hear an idea, ponder it, decide if it's true, and then form a hypothesis. But that is not how the brain works. Instead, we hear an idea, immediately decide it is true with our System 1 brain, and maybe later shift to System 2 thinking and vet the idea.

Beliefs, in turn, are based on facts and predictions. Our ability to process facts and make predictions is compromised. Annie points to confirmation bias, motivated reasoning, and tribe identification as three of the most pernicious ways the inputs that form our beliefs can be flawed. Confirmation bias is a well-known behavioral flaw that we notice and emphasize information that confirms our existing point of view. Michael Mauboussin said, "If you're in the investing business and you haven't fallen for confirmation bias, you're not doing your job." Motivated reasoning is confirmation bias on steroids. Investors work incredibly hard to discredit information that is contradictory to their hypothesis. Lastly, our affiliation with tribes influences our views. As an investor, we might be a card-carrying member of the value investing tribe, the trend following tribe, or the long-term investor tribe. We don't trust information from sources that arise from outside of our tribe.

Just becoming aware of our biases isn't enough to allay the pattern. We suffer from resulting, self-serving, and hindsight biases that inhibit our ability to improve our decision-making process. Annie refers to "resulting" as the inability to separate a good decision from a good outcome when assessing others. When allocators see good performance from a manager, they think the manager has made good decisions; bad performance must come from a bad decisions. As Paul Isaac of Arbiter Partners mocks managers, "volatility is only downside deviation. Upside deviation is called performance." All investors have a self-serving bias that wants to take credit when good things happen and defer blame when bad outcomes arise. It takes System 2 thinking to investigate when a bad outcome came out of a good decision process, and is even harder to recognize when dumb luck caused a good outcome to arise from a bad process. Hindsight bias gets in the way of accurately assessing past decisions. Investors subconsciously change the facts that led to decisions. Allocators are intelligent and thoughtful, which unfortunately only serves to strengthen their resolve. The smarter they are, the better they are at rationalizing existing beliefs, perfecting motivated reasoning, and sticking to opinions.

Investing in managers has less time pressure than a round of poker. While one might think allocators can mitigate these issues, even decisions without a timeline are biased.

Making good decisions as a team or with a committee compounds the challenge. Group dynamics can impinge independent thinking and truth discovery, two of the most important prerequisites for making good decisions.

CIOs generally work with teams, so let's turn to some steps to improve the decision-making process in a group setting.

Making better decisions

I have good news and bad news to share.

Let's start with the bad news. We are hardwired to make bad decisions even after we learn all the ways we are conditioned to muck it up. No matter how many times we read Kahneman's book, or how many times we listen to Annie on the podcast, we will still make the same mistakes. Drew Dickson of Albert Bridge Capital is keenly aware of this fact, cleverly articulated in the quote at the top of the chapter. But his knowledge of it alone won't change how he makes decisions.

Take a deep breath.

The good news is this awareness compels us to design systems that help mitigate the problem. We cannot change how our brain works, but we can think about information in a new way by striving to find an accurate representation of the truth and recognizing that we will only experience one of many outcomes that might occur. These two mental models open us to uncertainty, reduce overconfidence, and encourage contrary opinions.

CIOs can focus on two broad areas to improve their decision-making process. First, they can carefully design the structure of the team. Once this is done, they can add steps to their decision process to increase the probability of making good decisions.

1. Structure

Setting up the structure of the team lays the groundwork for a sound decision-making process. Teams can be more effective than individuals in unearthing and calibrating a range of possible outcomes in an investment decision. *Can be* is an important caveat, as a group that is constructed or managed poorly will exacerbate behavioral biases.

The size, continuity, and diversity of teams each have a substantial impact on a CIO's decision-making effectiveness.

a. Optimal size

Most CIOs oversee small teams internally. Boards can range in size. Michael Mauboussin cites research that the optimal size of a decision-making unit is four to six people. Annie Duke adds that a team of as little as three can be highly effective.

b. Continuity

The longer a team stays together, the better a CIO can function as a decision maker. More repetitions allow a team to develop institutional knowledge and grow confidence in their decision-making process. CIOs that have the ability and wherewithal to retain key team members, like David Swensen and Scott Malpass, have been some of the most successful over time.

c. Cognitive diversity

An ideal team has cognitive diversity, benefitting from members who think differently. Cognitively diverse team members may come from different backgrounds, training, experiences, and personalities. Social diversity (race, gender, age, ethnicity) may offer a wide range of life experiences and perspectives. Interestingly, social diversity does not result in cognitive diversity all the time. The key to good decision-making is fostering a team whose members think differently, not who look different but think the same way.

CIOs walk a thin line between the salutary benefit of different thinkers and the potential challenge of team cohesion. Cognitive diversity necessarily brings together team members from different tribes, who may instinctively be biased against each other's opinions due to differing norms of conduct. Ash Fontana at Zetta Ventures tries to find people to bring onto the team that are as different as they can possibly manage culturally.

Bridging this gap between diversity and cohesiveness is a challenge. Michael Mauboussin suggests seeking individuals with a high RQ, or rationality quotient. Rational thinkers are more adept at accepting differences in order to gain from the benefits of cognitive diversity. Gathering a team of high RQ, cognitively diverse people gets the ball rolling. The way the group takes shape determines its success.

2. Conduct

Once constructed, the course of conduct significantly influences how teams perform. Sound decision processes encourage cognitive safety, independence of thought, and behavioral awareness.

a. Cognitive safety

Team members need to feel safe in their role to verbalize divergent opinions. Much of this safety comes from the leader of the team, who sets the tone through their words and actions. Ana Marshall at the William and Flora Hewlett Foundation opens her team to expressing independent views by reminding them to "argue as if you're right, listen as if you're wrong, and be willing to change your mind."

The rest of the team consciously and subconsciously pays close attention. Effective leaders invite collaboration, encourage out-of-the-box thinking, and avoid blaming others for bad outcomes that follow good processes.

b. Independence of thought

The sequence of conversation in a group decision process can significantly alter the outcome. When a leader is respected or a perceived expert expresses an opinion, the rest of the team's otherwise independent views get compromised. If a venture capital specialist weighs in on the outstanding opportunity to invest with a new manager, other members of the team are more likely to defer to the specialist's opinion and withhold reservations they may have.

Effective leaders manage the potential to infect others with their beliefs through their orchestration of meetings. First, they allow the most junior or least informed team member to go first. Second, they steer the conversation away from more charismatic extroverts in the group, enabling introverts to have equal participation. Third, they withhold their view until others in the group have an opportunity to weigh in.

Fourth, they communicate in probabilities to express uncertainty and invite input. Lastly, they use a ballot voting system to avoid social proof when it comes time to weigh in on a decision.

c. Behavioral awareness

Each team member brings biases to the table. Teams that understand each other's individual biases are more effective at getting to the heart of issues without interference.

Kim Lew asks each of her team members to create a list of what gets in their way of objectively looking at investments. Where are they willing to take excessive risk, or why might they miss out on opportunities they should pursue? She also asks her team to come up with ideas to help them balance out these biases. Someone who is overconfident in a certain asset class may need a devil's advocate. Someone could be risk-averse and need encouragement in their convictions. When team members become aware of each other's biases, they can work together to form better decisions.

Noting other common biases can help CIOs avoid decision-making roadblocks. CIOs combat the natural instinct to give more credibility within a tribe by separating the quality of an idea from the deliverer of the idea. They can monitor how team members instinctively handle bad outcomes in an effort to focus on facts and away from emotions.

3. Thought process

Once the structure and norms of conduct for the team is in place, CIOs can turn to a checklist of considerations to organize investment decisions. These include thinking probabilistically, incorporating base rates, conducting risk assessments, checking biases, and eliciting feedback.

a. Think in probabilities

Effective teams speak in probabilities. In *Thinking in Bets*, Annie Duke recommends the phrase "Wanna bet?" for occasions when someone states an opinion as a fait accompli. Challenging someone to a bet holds them accountable in a way that normally does not happen. They instinctively shift from System 1 to System 2 thinking and compel teammates to move from certainty to uncertainty. Bob Rubin had a rule on his famed risk arbitrage desk at Goldman Sachs that no one could speak about an investment without framing the discussion with a probability tree of expected values.*

In *How to Decide*, Annie recommends a six-step decision process for making important decisions between two options. For each possibility, create a decision matrix that includes 1) all possible reasonable outcomes, 2) the payoffs of each, and 3) the probability of each occurring. Following these six steps encourages counterfactual thinking, where decision-makers broaden their perspective beyond the most probabilistic outcome to consider a range of possibilities.

b. Base rates

Incorporating base rates, or using the "outside view," is highly effective in reducing overconfidence.

Most of the time, we make investment decisions based on the "inside view." We gather information about an investment opportunity, dive into due diligence, use our experience and judgement, and make an assessment about the future.

Alternately, the outside view considers a statistical sample of similar past situations. Rather than assign expected returns and risks to one opportunity, an allocator studies a large group of similar opportunities in the past to put the decision in perspective.

For example, consider an analyst forecast for Amazon stock. The analyst believes Amazon will grow revenues by 15% per year for the next ten years and creates an amazingly detailed model to describe how Amazon will get there. Amazon has grown faster than that for a long time, so anchoring to recent history makes the model appear sensible.

However, the base rate for Amazon's future sales might look at every company since 1950 that has had $100 billion or more in revenue, adjusted for inflation, and ask how those companies grew in the subsequent ten years. It turns out there are 313 companies in that sample set and exactly

---

* The desk spawned a legacy of hedge fund titans, including Tom Steyer (Farallon Capital), Richard Perry (Perry Capital), Frank Brosens (Taconic Capital), Dan Och (Sculptor Management), Eric Mindich (Eton Park Capital), and Eddie Lampert (ESL Investments).

zero of them grew at 15% annually from that large a revenue base. Only seven grew more than 10% per annum, or 2% of the total in the reference class. It is certainly possible that Amazon will grow at 15% for the next ten years, but the base rate of 0% might inform the analyst that their model has a lower probability of hitting the revenue target than they initially projected from their inside view.

Base rates are helpful for allocators both in their own investment decisions and in assessing the decisions of managers. Allocators tend to put little weight on the outside view of managers, relying instead on their assessment of individuals in their analysis. Many CIOs are excited about the hedge funds in their portfolio yet are pessimistic about the average hedge fund return. Incorporating base rates into the research process can prove helpful in cooling overconfident expectations.

Additionally, allocators can consider managers' use of base rates in their due diligence. Managers that consider both the outside view and inside view in their security selection are likely to make better decisions over time. Those unfamiliar with the concept may have a blind spot.

c. Risk assessments

When the investment case to underwrite a manager is complete, CIOs can take a step back and reconsider what might go wrong. Pre-mortem analysis, red teams, devil's advocates, and pro-con lists all help unearth risks the CIO may not have considered when building their thesis.

1. Pre-mortem analysis

Gary Klein is a cognitive psychologist who studies how professionals become highly skilled at their craft. He created the pre-mortem analysis to help fighter pilots in the air force. A pre-mortem is a risk management tool that moves up a post-mortem analysis chronologically to uncover alternative possibilities that may not have been considered.

An example process for a pre-mortem is shown here.

a. "The plan has failed."

The CIO kicks off the pre-mortem by telling the team they have looked in a crystal ball and seen that the plan has failed. Framing the conversation this way, as opposed to asking "What could go wrong?", changes the mindset to see a disaster and own it. The counterfactual allows the brain to access thinking and speculation that it would not otherwise engage.

b. Take a pause

The CIO gives the team a few seconds to sit with this reality. The plan has failed.

c. Write down what happened

Each team member individually takes two minutes to write down all the reasons why the plan has failed. Two minutes affords them enough time to think, but not so much time that the energy in the room is lost. Writing down ideas encourages independent thought.

d. Share ideas one at a time, starting with the leader

The leader begins sharing ideas for why the plan has failed. In starting out, the leader purposely infects the group in taking the exercise seriously. The rest of the team will follow suit.

The leader calls on team members one at a time, requiring each team member to share one potential problem with the plan. The format encourages introverts to speak out and controls extroverts from dominating the discussion. It fosters cognitive safety and gives permission for everyone to bring up ideas.

The leader continues to orchestrate a flow around the table until the team has presented all of its ideas.

e. Write down actions to mitigate risk

Seeing everything that can go wrong, the team then takes two more minutes to write down all of the ways they individually can prevent these outcomes from occurring.

f. Share risk prevention actions

The CIO initiates a round of hearing what can be done to mitigate the risks presented.

g. End meeting

The CIO adjourns the meeting, steps back and thinks about the decision, now armed with an additional array of information. They can reassess the decision and make a new plan of action using all the material unearthed in the pre-mortem.

Pre-mortems reduce overconfidence of decisions more than any other technique, foster a culture of candor, and makes teams smarter.

2. Red teams

Andy Golden utilizes "red teams," in which a distinct group is tasked with conducting research and poking holes in the recommendation made by the recommending "blue team." Red teaming is more time-intensive than a pre-mortem and requires more resources.

Red teams also bring along a host of potential biases. Team leaders again need to ensure independence of thought and cognitive safety. Importantly, the red team must take ownership of their role. Red and blue team members are typically part of the same organization, a tribe of its own. The approach loses effectiveness if the red team holds back on their critique. Red teams are most effective when the individuals come with different areas of expertise and are not personally invested in the recommendation.

3. Other risk management tools

Devil's advocate and *pro/con lists* are other tools that can be used to unearth contrary states of the world. A devil's advocate is tasked with poking holes in a thesis. Red teams generally are more effective than devil's advocates. The devil's advocate approach loses the cognitive diversity of the whole group and can get antagonistic. However, when teams are constrained by resources, devil's advocates can add a valuable step to the investment process.

Listing out positives and negatives of a decision – a pro/con list – is a reasonable starting point. This is better than not considering alternatives at all, but Gary Klein's research discovered that a list of cons is less effective than pre-mortems in tapping into the creativity of the team.

d. Bias checklist

CIOs can use a checklist at the point of decision to review common biases. Timing and overconfidence are two examples that tend to afflict investment decisions.

Ostensibly, all investment research concludes that individuals and institutions chase performance. We tend to invest in managers or buy securities after strong periods of returns and redeem or sell after periods of weakness. We can create a high-functioning team, consider base rates, conduct pre-mortems, and still make decisions that chase performance. Separating the decision about investing with a manager from the timing in doing so when permittable is a helpful trick to mitigate the bias. Getting excited about a manager need not equate to investing immediately when the enthusiasm takes hold.

CIOs and their teams are rarely more enthusiastic about a manager than the first day they put capital to work. Their team has put significant time and effort into research and is deeply vested in the new relationship. Optimism runs high and overconfidence can easily creep into their thinking. We broadly tend to overestimate a manager's edge and underestimate the future volatility of a strategy at the moment of decision. Adding a check on position sizing can help combat this bias. Overconfidence may lead to sizing a position higher than would be warranted, whereas starting off conservatively allows a more realistic assessment of the future over time. Some investments offer the opportunity to cut losses as well, which can help prevent mistakes when we become emotionally unhinged.

e. Feedback loops

We can make very good decisions that do not work out. When I look back at my decision to bet with Warren Buffett, I still believe it followed a good process and the odds of winning were in my favor.

Alternatively, we can make terrible decisions that do work out. Annie Duke shared that her decision to quit academia to play poker came from one of the worst decision processes of her life.

Our natural tendency as individuals is to draw the wrong lessons from decisions: bad outcomes are not our fault and good outcomes come from good processes. Making better decisions requires feedback to evolve and enhance the investment process. Documenting decisions, creating a decision group, and considering the role of luck are useful tools to build feedback loops in the decision process.

1. Decision journal

Improving the investment process requires an accurate statement of the facts and beliefs known at the time the decision gets made. Hindsight bias will cloud our memory of what we knew. A decision journal ensures a CIO can learn and grow from a review of past decisions.

Part of my conviction in the quality of my decision to bet with Buffett comes from a white paper I wrote at the time of the bet. I based my assessment of the probability of success on an outside view of the wager – the S&P 500 had never before outperformed the hedge fund index over a ten-year period. However, I did not conduct a pre-mortem, which may have unearthed the possibility of markets shifting and lowered my conviction.

Annie had no such process when she moved from the academic world to poker. She looks back and thinks she barely even made a conscious decision to play poker in the first place. It was the only path that came up and she just went with it. Hence why she recalls it now as a terrible decision process.

2. Convene a decision group

A CIO can address *decision washing* by leaning on others in a decision group.

An effective decision group follows the structure and conduct principles above, ensuring open and frank communication. The group seeks to discover the truth about a decision rather than to determine who was right.

Annie uses the acronym CUDOS to describe the characteristics of a good decision group.

> C: Communism – share all the data transparently, especially information that paints a view in a bad light.

> U: Universalism – seek the objective truth. Pay attention to the bias to overweight or dismiss facts depending on who is communicating the message.

D: Disinterested – note our emotional conflicts of interest. Be mindful of motivated reasoning, confirmation bias, and hindsight bias.

OS: Objective Skepticism – approach the world asking why things aren't true.

3. Role of luck

As the skill of managers increased over time, luck has become more important in outcomes. The dynamic pointed out by Michael Mauboussin has permeated investing just as it did with Major League Baseball hitters over the last few decades.

Money managers tend not to see the importance of luck in their success. Among the many managers Brian Portnoy met, he found that the vast majority would not accept that luck was part of the equation when their returns were strong. Good performance demonstrated skill, bad performance was bad luck: a textbook example of self-serving bias.

Allocators need to be patient and gather lots of information to distinguish between a manager's luck and skill. Tim Recker at the James Irvine Foundation reminds his team that business cycles can last seven to eight years, and some managers need a full business cycle to show that their strategy works.

Summary

Making good decisions is hard. We are hardwired to do this poorly, so building processes to mitigate our pernicious biases can help make our decisions *less bad*.

Investment ideas are not black and white. Known and unknown risks are a part of every investment, and it is rare to have an honest consensus on a team. When functioning at a high level, teams unearth many scenarios and assign probabilities to potential outcomes that provide the full mosaic of information for a CIO to decide.

When a CIO has made the decision to hire a manager, they may find they are a price-taker, needing to accept the terms offered by a manager in high demand from allocators. Other times, the CIO may be in position to negotiate terms. The next chapter discusses how to make the most out of those opportunities.

To learn more

Podcasts

Capital Allocators: Annie Duke – Improving Decision-Making (Ep.39)

Capital Allocators: Annie Duke – How to Decide (Ep.156)

Capital Allocators: Gary Klein with Paul Johnson and Paul Sonkin – Conducting Pre-Mortem Analysis (Ep.109)

Capital Allocators: Michael Mauboussin – Active Challenges, Rational Decisions and Team Dynamics (Ep.36)

Books

Thinking, Fast and Slow, Daniel Kahneman

Thinking in Bets, Annie Duke

How to Decide, Annie Duke

Chapter 3
Negotiations

"Negotiation is learning."

– Daylian Cain

CIOs are tasked with negotiating issues big and small. They embrace a partnership mentality and enjoy being on the same side of the table as their managers. After a lengthy discovery and due diligence process to identify a new manager, they often dread negotiating the terms of the relationship. Many are self-effacing about their inability to win a negotiation.

When leading their organization, CIOs regularly negotiate compensation, meeting attendees, and everything in between. As soon as the day is done, CIOs go home and encounter negotiations with family members too.

I got indoctrinated into the world of negotiations at business school. With teaching from *Getting Past No*[17] and *Getting to Yes*,[18] I learned about reaching an agreement where both sides feel good about the outcome. The theory involved acronyms like finding a ZOPA (zone of possible agreement), knowing your BATNA (best alternative to negotiated agreement), and managing emotions by "going to the balcony." We were told to focus on interests instead of positions, look for ways to "expand the pie," and put ourselves in our counterparty's shoes. I enjoyed thinking of the many efficient, positive, win-win negotiations in my future.

I proceeded to get steamrolled on every important negotiation I encountered.

Just as recognizing behavioral bias in making decisions is completely different from avoiding it, negotiations in practice are different from theory. Daylian Cain teaches negotiations in a practical way at Yale

University School of Management and offered some suggestions on the show to improve outcomes in all negotiations.

His lessons can be divided into preparation, updating views, and tricks of the trade.

Preparation

The biggest mistake negotiators make is inadequate preparation. Daylian conducts extensive experiments with his students. With great consistency, he finds that the most prepared students score the highest, irrespective of their prowess in the negotiation itself. Proper preparation includes assessing your interests, those of your counterparty, and contingency planning.

1. Your interests

Organize your thoughts with a planning document that answers the following questions:

What do you want?

Why do you want it?

What are your priorities?

What is your exchange rate?

What and why are straightforward. Planning gets tricky around priorities and exchange rates. Our top priorities are what we need out of the process; whereas, lower priorities may be sacrificed in order to achieve the most important goals.

Good planning considers the price of trade-offs, or the exchange rate. We don't place the same value on each priority and attaching numbers to outcomes turns implicit choices into explicit ones.

For example, if you are taking a job in a new location and are buying a house, consider the price of commuting. How much is it worth to add 15 minutes to a daily commute in order to buy more land or a bigger house? It may seem strange to put in monetary terms, but the house you choose to buy and the price you pay will do exactly that. We can either plan in advance to consciously price out our interests, or let the process unfold and have choices priced for us. In the context of investing, a CIO considers explicit trade-offs, like the appropriate fee discount for a longer-dated share class, and implicit ones, like the value of transparency.

2. Your counterparty's interests

The next aspect of planning is considering the same questions for your counterparty.

What do they want?

Why do they want it?

What are their priorities?

What is their exchange rate?

Most people don't learn enough about their counterparty before entering the negotiation. We can figure out our own interests with a little time and thought, but doing the same for a counterparty requires gathering information from others. Whether negotiating terms of a partnership or terms of a new job, we can find people who know more about our counterparty's needs and wants than we do.

Daylian suggests getting started learning about your counterparty's interests two weeks before the negotiation to allow for gathering data and reflecting on interests. Even if it proves challenging to learn specifics, spending time thinking about a counterparty's interests readies you to update and revise your views as the process unfolds.

3. Contingency planning

Many people enter negotiations preparing to take a victory lap. They understand everything they want, assume they will get it, and stop there. Their counterparty probably has prepared the exact same way. Actual negotiations encounter constraints that move both sides away from sweeping every consideration from the other.

Planning for contingencies maps out possible paths the negotiation might take. Think of the negotiation as a game of chess and consider what moves you want to make if your counterparty moves a pawn, a knight, or the queen. Working through many possible alternatives provides the most comprehensive approach to planning. The more you practice what you will say in different scenarios, the more prepared you will be for bumps in the road.

Updating views

Imagine a negotiation you enter with both your preparation sheet and your counterparty's sheet in hand. You have perfect information and will leave with everything you want inside the zone of agreement. The useful characteristics of a good negotiator that otherwise matter, like even-temperament, confidence, and relative bargaining power, pale in comparison to knowing exactly what your counterparty wants.

Once the negotiation begins, seek to continue learning about your counterparty. View the negotiation as a process of discovery instead of a battle. As you update your knowledge of their needs, priorities, and exchange rate, you move through the process guided by relevant facts.

There is only one way to do this: listening. Daylian's research shows that most people feel the need to talk and state their case in a negotiation, when listening is by far more effective in gaining an advantage.

Active listening in a negotiation is a variation of the theme for listening while conducting interviews, including noting, mirroring, validating, and empathising.

1. Noting distractions

Laying the groundwork for a successful negotiation requires calming your emotions. If you want your counterparty to talk, you need to make them feel safe. Start off grounded and clear-minded to create a space for your counterparty to feel the same way. Recognize when you get distracted and return to listening intently to pick up clues that your counterparty shares.

2. Mirroring

Mirroring simply and resisting the temptation to defend your position or solve problems is highly effective. Responses that help frame a mirror in negotiations include the following:

"Let me make sure I got that …"

"It sounds like …"

When you have finished the mirror, check in with the counterparty by asking "Did I hear you correctly?" or "Did I get that right?" and allow them to make corrections. Then mirror back those corrections.

3. Validating

Validating is especially tricky in a negotiation when opposing views trigger an emotional response. You may not agree with what your counterparty has said, but you can still validate their view by putting yourself in their shoes. Resist the temptation to argue or express your opinion before you validate their stance.

Expressions that help frame validation include the following:

"If you believe x, I can see the logic in what you're saying."

"Given that you think y, it makes sense that you would want z."

"Now that I hear you are saying x, it makes sense you would want z."

4. Empathizing and being curious

In some situations, expressing emotional empathy can move a sticky process forward. For those who can't imagine engaging in this touchy-feely realm, Daylian suggests replacing the notion of empathy with curiosity. Be curious about what your counterparty wants in your exploration of their interest. With either mindset of empathy or curiosity, you move away from focusing on differences and set aside counterattacking, talking about yourself, or disagreeing.

Additional tips

Preparation, updating views, and the language of communication are important prerequisites in the negotiation process. Daylian also offers a set of seven actionable tips that help along the way.

1. Knowing your worth

Counterparties in a negotiation rarely have equal bargaining power. A CIO may oversee a big pool of capital and engage with a start-up fund with few suitors. A venture capital firm may have limited capacity and significant excess demand from investors.

The more powerful player often goes after a proportional share of the pie. My business school course in negotiations taught the theory of expanding the pie, which encourages counterparties to find ways to increase the size of the pie instead of debating how to carve up a fixed pie.

Daylian teaches the smaller player to identify the unique synergies of the deal and work to split those synergies in half. Unique synergies are those that can't be obtained without each other. Importantly, describing the concept of unique synergies is not what leads larger counterparties to offer more than a proportional share. It is the economic value of the synergies that does the trick. The smaller player is essential in creating those synergies and need not accept only a proportional share of the benefits.

2. Non-monetary terms

Money is the driver of business and investment negotiations. It has value to both sides and is a win-lose proposition. A laser focus on financial considerations can lose sight of non-monetary terms that also have value. Search for non-financial benefits to bring more value into the discussion.

3. Smart trades

Negotiation inevitably involves give and take. Rather than trying to split every issue down the middle, look for terms that are big wins for one side and small losses for the other. A series of smart trades can add meaningful value to both sides.

4. Contingent agreements

Counterparties often have different outlooks of the future. The seller of a business may believe in a faster rate of organic growth than the buyer does. The buyer may believe its distribution network will expand growth more than the seller does.

Contingent agreements allow counterparties to resolve differences about the future. Deals to sell a business frequently have earnouts, where the performance of the business after the closing determines the ultimate price paid.

5. Going first

Behavioral psychology suggests that making the first offer benefits from anchoring. Daylian believes the research on the order of operations is inconclusive. If you go first without sufficient information about your counterparty's interest, you will wave your finger in thin air and may unknowingly anchor too low. Going first and anchoring high is effective only when you have learned as much as possible about the zone of agreement.

6. Labelling

At sticky times in a negotiation, using soft language can help keep both sides engaged. In *Never Split the Difference*,[19] former hostage negotiator Chris Voss discusses the importance of relabeling the word "No." Turning a negative into a further exploration can turn a deal breaker into a deal maker. He suggests phrases to move the ball forward:

"What about this doesn't work for you?"

"What would you need to make this work?"

7. Walking Away

Walking away from an agreement puts pressure on the counterparty to reconsider their position. At times, walking away with a graceful path to re-enter the negotiation can be the most valuable tool.

Daylian literally can't get his students to walk away. He described a negotiations class in which he made walking away at least once during the semester a requirement to pass the class. Even then, half of his students hadn't walked away going into the last negotiation session. He reminded them that they needed to just walk away and come back. Knowing a passing grade was on the line, they still didn't do it.

Walking away creates anxiety and risks leaving value behind in the pursuit of more. However, it is a highly successful tactic to extract just that.

Summary

Negotiations are a necessary part of investing, running an investment organization, and life. Preparing, updating information, and communicating effectively can enable CIOs to deliver more value for their constituents.

The skills of interviewing, decision-making, and negotiating position a CIO to be able to implement their investment strategy. Most do not work alone, so understanding how to lead a team is essential to making it all come together.

To learn more

Podcasts

Capital Allocators: Daylian Cain – Master Class in Negotiations (Ep.138)

The Knowledge Project: Chris Voss – The Art of Letting Other People Have Your Way (Ep.27)

Online course

Negotiation Mind Games, Daylian Cain, www.negotiationmindgames.com.

Books

Never Split the Difference, Chris Voss

Chapter 4
Leadership

"Successful investors are brilliant, focused, and hard working with tremendous insights that rarely extend to managing people."

— Jon Hirtle

CIOs have two full-time jobs: managing a pool of capital and managing a team of people. Few CIOs are trained in leading people as they rise through the ranks. Apprenticeship in the business teaches the skills to grow financial capital far more than the skills to lead human capital.

I have worked with some great money managers and colleagues, but the only lessons I learned about leadership and managing others came through osmosis. My colleagues, in turn, had never learned the disciplines either. As a result, many of my lessons were observations about what not to do.

CIOs have to learn how to lead a team. A few of the guests on the show specialize in leadership and learned their craft in other disciplines. Michael Lombardi, football coach and commentator, had the benefit of working for Bill Walsh and Bill Belichick. David "Bull" Gurfein, leadership coach, was a career military veteran ensconced in leadership training. And Jeff Solomon of Cowen Inc., describes lessons he learned from his time at summer camp:

> You end up in a cabin with a bunch of people and you have to make it work. It's all day, every day, 24-hours a day. Sometimes that can be super hard, but you've got to make it work because you don't have a choice. You learn how to fit in with a group, how to play with a group, how to find people you like and manage around people you don't. Some days at summer camp, it's just about getting to the end of the day and having fun. Those are

basic skills at the center of human interaction in groups, and you learn that at places like summer camp.

The tools these leaders describe offer a common framework in leadership training. Great leaders adopt the following rules of thumb:

- Define a vision
- Set standards of conduct
- Communicate consistently and frequently
- Behave authentically
- Inspire and motivate
- Adapt and evolve

Define a vision

Successful leadership starts with defining a focused vision for the organization – the "why" in Simon Sinek's lexicon.[20] Effective leaders create the vision, articulate it repeatedly and passionately, and believe in it deeply.

The vision is a key driver of culture, which we know, feel, and embrace even if it's elusive to define. It permeates the company from hiring decisions to investment decisions. A clearly defined mission will attract like-minded employees and inspire enthusiasm and commitment from them. The leader motivates the team by helping them believe they are part of something bigger than themselves and their daily work.

Greg Fleming from Rockefeller Capital Management observed business leaders early in his career as a management consultant and found the most successful ones had a vision that is tight, clear, and communicated constantly. For example, Bob Iger, the retired CEO of Disney, described his vision for the company when he took the reins as "create high-quality, branded content, embrace technology, and globalize the business."[21] That vision became the leading light of the company ever since, informing everything from acquisition strategy to internal objectives.

Bull Gurfein is a decorated marine veteran. From an early age, he was trained to be a leader with lives on the line. He defines leadership as "a trust, a bond, a set of principles that cover the basics of formulating plans and understanding how to give orders." The vision in the Marines is called the Commander's Intent. For each mission, the commander describes the who, what, where, when, why, and how. The Commander's Intent is the why and how: why is the mission happening and how should the unit conduct themselves to get it done.

Michael Lombardi delineates the success of sustainable-based leaders over solution-based leaders. Sustainable-based leaders have a vision that thinks about the long term; whereas, solution-based leaders shift around their vision to address more immediate issues.

Jen Prosek, the leader of her eponymous public relations firm, calls her team "The Army of Entrepreneurs." In the turn of a phrase, she expresses a vision for sustainable leadership.

Patrick O'Shaughnessy created the phrase "Learn, Build, Share, Repeat" to define the vision for O'Shaughnessy Asset Management. That vision encompasses all aspects of the quantitative research and software platform. Team members are expected to continuously learn, take a role in building new products or services or enhancing existing functionality, share those findings with clients and the community, and do that over and over again. It is easy to imagine a culture of knowledge and practice following that vision.

Jeff Solomon's motto for Cowen is "Vision, Tenacity, and Empathy." Those words speak volumes about what differentiates Cowen from other financial services organizations. Tenacity might be a common Wall Street stereotype. Vision implies an entrepreneurial mindset that might be different from functionally siloed organizations. Empathy is out of the realm of expectations. The combination of the three is special and has proven emblematic of a unique culture and character of the people under his watch.

A vision sets the tone for organizations to align. Following and communicating the vision are required to keep it alive.

Set standards of conduct

John Wooden, UCLA's legendary basketball coach, famously dedicated the first day of practice every year to teaching his players how to properly tie their shoes. By meticulously learning the most basic step in getting ready to play, his players understood that attention to detail in every facet of the game was the standard expected of them by Coach Wooden.

After establishing a vision, leaders create expectations for how members of the team should behave and perform. Importantly, a team will follow a leader's actions more than their words: walking the walk dominates talking the talk. Coach Wooden made a point in his first practice, but his players would soon forget the lesson if he showed up every day looking dishevelled with untied shoelaces himself. By practicing what he preached every day, the impeccably dressed leader reinforced his message.[22]

Leaders demonstrate the culture through their actions. They determine the pace of activity, degree of intensity, method of communication, respect of others' time, and a host of intangibles that permeate the organization.

Michael Lombardi described the habits of Patriots coach Bill Belichick and 49ers coach Bill Walsh in reverent terms. Belichick has meticulous work habits that are productive and efficient. His schedule to prepare for each game starts shortly after the prior game ends and is organized down to the hour from early in the morning until late at night every week during the season. Walsh set clear objectives to be courteous, seek knowledge, and stay current. His standards of excellence were expected equally from the offensive coordinator to the janitorial staff.

Chatri Sityodtong uses the "warrior spirit" known throughout the mixed martial arts community as the standard of conduct at ONE Championship. Warrior spirit describes grit, perseverance, and willpower to conquer adversity. In his business, as in his physical training, he describes mistakes as getting knocked down. No matter what, he always gets back up. The metaphor flows through to intellectual honesty, which he believes is the bedrock for continuous learning. Staying humble, admitting mistakes, and learning from the team allows each employee at ONE Championship to follow the martial arts motto of trying to improve by 1% every day.

Greg Fleming often repeats a quote from Packers great Vince Lombardi that suggests an expectation for his team. "Perfection is not attainable; but if we chase it, we might just catch excellence." He doesn't just talk the talk, as his executive team relates that he commonly sends emails with new ideas and follow-ups on deliverables before 6 a.m. Greg also believes in decentralizing decision-making and giving talented people the autonomy to act. He focuses his time on finding great people, agreeing on a path, and empowering them to run with it.

The Marine Corps has a clearly defined code of conduct that empowers troops. As Bull Gurfein describes, "troops eat first." The perspective of the Marine Corps is an inverted pyramid, where the leader is at the bottom trying to balance everything. Success in the battlefield comes from an 18-year-old rifleman who must locate, close-in, and defeat the enemy, not the Lieutenant Colonel setting the Commander's Intent. Leadership is disseminated across the entire organization. Whether a troop in the field or a cook at the barracks, Marines repeat the phrase "We Are Marines." This defines them holistically.

Mission statements adorn the walls of many investment offices around the world. While admirable in intent, most mission statements turn into empty words. The articulated expression of a code of conduct gets put to the test when conflicts arise. The degree to which leaders articulate and incorporate "integrity," "communication" or "teamwork" in year-end bonuses or hiring decisions will determine whether the mission statement on the wall has any teeth. Actual norms and standards of conduct follow from decisions made in these moments. Nicely decorated artwork gets devalued immediately and forever unless hard choices made by leaders are consistent with the stated mission.

Communicate consistently and frequently

Successful leaders reiterate their vision and live up to their espoused standards of conduct. It is top of mind for leaders all the time and flows seamlessly in their words and behavior.

Michael Lombardi offers a framework called ROMPS to consider when communicating with a team:

RO: Room – Command the room

M: Message – Command the message

P: Process – Command the process

S: Self – Command yourself

Commanding the room is about presence, including body language, tone of voice, and confidence. *Commanding the message* is the ability to explain the plan with one consistent voice across the organization. Each team member should be able to effortlessly repeat the vision and standards of conduct. *Commanding the process* involves waking up every morning committed to the culture. Lastly, *commanding yourself* entails living up to the standards you set for others, including self-discipline, education, and growth. These ROMPS nicely bind together the principles of vision, standards, and communication.

Greg Fleming commonly reminds his team that "it takes a village." He believes that organizations that are successful in the long term rely on the entire team to reach their goals. The cliché about raising a child is consistent with his standard of conduct for empowering the team.

Jen Prosek has a gift for creating catchphrases that reinforce the vision for her army of entrepreneurs. She encourages the team to "Just Ask" for new business. She holds regular team meetings to offer availability and transparency, including the "J Low Down" when anyone can ask and get answers to any question about the business. She also articulated her vision in a book, *Army of Entrepreneurs*, that explores an owner's mindset and describes her methods to attract, motivate, train, reward, and retain the members of her team.[23]

Jeff Solomon reinforces empathy as a unique characteristic of Cowen in his daily demeanor. He has an innate ability to sit in other people's shoes and has a warm, welcoming tone of voice. Jeff harkens back to his summer camp experience and tells his team that when things get tough, which they inevitably will, they can sit down and say "Hey, we are on the same team and trying to accomplish the same thing. Let's talk about why we're arguing because if we're arguing because we have different ideas on how to get to a common goal, let's focus on the common goal."

Leaders who communicate effectively do so with authenticity, which in turn allows them to inspire and motivate their team.

Behave authentically

Self-awareness and humility are essential characteristics of successful leaders. Thomas DeLong, Professor of Organizational Behavior at Harvard Business School, believes leadership is deeply personal.

Thomas spent eight years side-by-side with John Mack when John led Morgan Stanley. Thomas saw very bright, technically competent, high-need-for-achievement individuals thirsting for honest conversations.

He sought to develop managers who enable other people to experience themselves more fully and better when in their presence. That process starts with an exploration of the self, talking to yourself to settle down, quiet the mind, and be available for others.

The deep honesty Thomas sought goes hand in hand with humility and vulnerability.

When Jen Prosek instructs her army to "Just Ask," she teaches that the right way to approach a sale is with humanity. Be humble, straightforward, and bring common sense.

Inspire and motivate

Leaders need to motivate and inspire their team with their words and actions. Their modus operandi will set the tone for the organization. Great leaders energize their team to achieve more than they realize is possible.

Admired Leadership founder Randall Stutman has coached 12,000 leaders and found a universal frame for leaders to make people feel special. Team members are all different. Some are motivated by financial rewards and others by mastery of a subject, belonging, or serving a higher purpose. Trying to motivate each team member according to their specific needs gets complicated quickly. Instead, great leaders can act like a fan – clapping, cheering, and rooting for their team and demonstrating they are willing to do anything to help each team member succeed in good times and bad. The concept of *fanness* is a consistent, highly effective leadership trait across all of Randall's work.[24] Each of the following examples are forms of fanness.

Greg Fleming believes in positive motivation and upbeat morale. He points to the importance of optimism, describing it as true moral courage. When he thinks about inspiring his team, Greg focuses on the particular strengths of individuals. He takes people who are good and wants to make them feel great and have a sense of purpose. In order to move the collective organization forward, Greg wants each teammate to feel stimulated and excited when they get off the elevator each morning.

Jen Prosek also inspires through optimism. She carries herself with a smile on her face and supports her team with positivity. She recites the phrase from Ella Wheeler Wilcox, "Laugh and the world laughs with you. Weep and you weep alone," to remind those around her that the world wants to associate with those who have passion and energy. She then supports her team by fostering that positive energy, citing phrases like "Let your enemy be your energy."

Chatri Sityodtong inspires his team through his own warrior spirit. He repeatedly shares his personal story and ignites passion through his actions, reinforcing the warrior spirit and acting as a perpetual student.

Jeff Solomon articulates his passion for empathy as his guiding leadership light. As he describes the powerful force:

> You need to understand what motivates the person you're trying to engage with. You don't have to agree with it; you just need to understand it. And the best way to understand how somebody thinks or what motivates them is to try and imagine what it's like to be them.
>
> I want to know what you care about most. Why are you doing what you're doing? When you ask questions like that from clients, a lot of times you'll hear answers that you would agree with.
>
> Managing is all about saying, I feel you, and I think I can be helpful. And, by the way, you know, there's an economic trade in there too. Can I move the needle for you, and can we move the needle for each other? Can I lend my brand to enhance your opportunity set? Can we affiliate with one another to get to a better spot than we were?
>
> I don't discount the fact that they're individuals, and they want to succeed on their own. I just want to be the enabler. If they value enablement, if they value the way that we permission them with tools and products and services and relationships, they can be better here than anywhere else. But they're still individuals who want to win desperately. That is the essence of teamwork.

Adapt and evolve

Leaders embrace change. As Michael Lombardi puts it, "If you don't like change, you're going to like irrelevance even less." The best laid plans can go awry, and even a well-defined vision may need updating and adapting as the world evolves.

Early warnings of the need to change course can come from feedback loops internally and externally. When Bull Gurfein steps into an organization to consult management, he asks three questions of every person:

> What are we doing right?
>
> What are we doing wrong?
>
> What could we be doing better?

Leaders as sole individuals can miss important trends happening within their organization, with clients, and in the industry. By getting feedback and doing more of what is going right, cutting out what is going wrong, and improving on what needs to be done better, leaders can detect necessary changes and set a path to communicating a change in course when necessary.

When the time comes to make changes, Thomas DeLong suggests starting small. Inertia is a powerful force and people do not naturally embrace change. By finding small wins and easily digestible movements in a different direction, the team can begin a process of changing direction behind the leader.

Summary

Leadership entails setting a vision, regularly reminding the team of that vision, taking actions that are aligned with the vision, and being a fan of team members. Great CIOs are talented both in investing and leadership, crafting and fostering a vision aligned with their goals.

When a CIO sets a path to follow a vision, they then must ensure the vision is executed by the team. Let's turn to some lessons in managing people.

To learn more

Podcasts

Capital Allocators: Jennifer Prosek – Branding an Asset Management Firm (Ep.81)

Capital Allocators: Randall Stutman – Admired Leadership (Ep.150)

Online course

Admired Leadership, Randall Stutman and the Admired Leadership team

Randall and his team discuss 100 universal behaviors of admired leaders that they uncovered in their work. It is the best, most actionable set of tools I have come across. Available at www.admiredleadership.com.

Books

The Ride of a Lifetime, Bob Iger

Army of Entrepreneurs, Jennifer Prosek

It is a folly for me to try to recommend leadership books. Instead, I have shared two that struck me as being true to the lessons in this chapter.

Chapter 5

Management

"Our job is to manage people's time, give them the ability to be successful, help them prioritize, develop clear guidelines and plans, and create timelines with milestones and objectives."

– Bull Gurfein

If leadership is the vision, management is the implementation of the vision. Money managers have a reputation for being less talented with people than with capital. Managing people takes time away from other activities, so it is an area that is often overlooked. It requires training and experience commonly left out of investment organizations.

Managing others requires a CIO to go from being a great individual contributor to overseeing the contributions of others. The transition requires delegating, giving feedback, and allowing subordinates to make mistakes and learn. Scott Kupor from Andreessen Horowitz describes the job of a manager as keeping the trains moving, giving people direction, and answering questions.

Basic management techniques sound like common sense once shared. The processes include the following:

- Hiring
- Organizational design
- Project management
- Talent development
- Time management

Hiring

In both hiring money managers and executing a strategy, the importance of great people ranks at the top of most checklists. Chatri Sityodtong says it well in proclaiming, "to unleash your greatness, surround yourself with greatness." At the same time, defining what constitutes a great team member differs in each leader's mind.

Managing people begins with the hiring process. Many recruiting processes lack structure, defaulting to candidates with the requisite professional skills and a similar personality to the interviewer. Instead, job interviewing can share a similar process to manager interviews, starting with a strategy for everyone involved to follow.

The team can prepare probing, open-ended questions that focus on different aspects of a candidate's character, and use a scorecard to rank desired traits. A good process considers the candidate's goals, including financial, cultural, and developmental, as well as those of the organization.

The interviewing process at WCM Investment Management exemplifies this discipline. Culture is a driving force in the success of the firm. Paul Black stresses the importance of a great culture internally and a culture aligned with competitive advantage in their portfolio companies. WCM's interview process separates the core attributes the firm believes are required for a candidate to thrive. In each interview, a WCM team member focuses on assessing one of those characteristics. Together, the series of interviews paints a full picture of the candidate.

Wellington Management is proud of its track record of infrequent hiring mistakes when bringing in talent. Its collaborative culture and merit-based private ownership model necessitates a working environment where expectations are high and people care about each other.

Jim Williams focuses on five key areas to explore in job interviews, which he notes are also important topics for manager interviews:

1. Smart

Problem solving and street smarts. Questions focus on examples of problems they have solved.

2. Communication

Both oral and written. The process includes samples.

3. Team player

Those willing to share what they know. Questions focus on examples of team projects.

4. Integrity

People who take responsibility and make decisions because it is the right thing to do. Questions inquire about situations where something went wrong.

5. Experience

Relevant experience for the role.

Jim notes these traits are essential to draw out of candidates in advance, because only the last one, experience, will change over time. He encourages his team to let the interview flow naturally as a conversation where they eventually cover all of these topics.

After hiring hundreds of portfolio managers and operations professionals over 20 years in the hedge fund business, Jason Karp of HumanCo categorizes hires in three buckets: dangerous, nuisance, and good.[25] His taxonomy is an insightful framework for hiring.

Dangerous hires love following the herd. They are intellectually dishonest and have difficulty admitting mistakes or changing their mind when the facts change. Dangerous hires fall victim to most behavioral biases, confuse process with outcome, express overconfidence, rely excessively on gut feel, mix facts and opinions, and fail to learn from mistakes. The work of dangerous hires lacks detail and focuses too much on the big picture. Culturally, dangerous hires can be toxic to an organization with cancerous complaining and subverting of others.

Dangerous hires pose a severe risk to a business, especially smaller organizations where each person matters. Jason suggests looking for signs of issues in their personal life, including a lack of impulse control and discipline.

Nuisance hires are less dangerous, but still pose challenges. These people can be annoying and suffer from poor communication skills. They tend to blame others when something goes wrong and dwell on failure instead of success. On the investing front, nuisance hires lack original ideas, have low conviction, and cower in the face of adversity. Managing nuisance hires requires a lot of time and generates a low return on that time. These people pose a lower risk to the business, but create large opportunity costs.

Good hires bring positive optionality and are wonderful investments for an organization. These select people are intellectually honest and willing to change their mind easily when warranted. They are competitive, self-motivated, overachieving, ambitious, and gritty. As individuals, they have a thirst for self-improvement and introspection, take true accountability, and engage in a deliberate practice to learn and grow. As a member of a team, good hires demonstrate high EQ and outstanding interpersonal communication. In their personal lives, they are disciplined risk-takers and show evidence of willpower. When managers find these good people, they invest the time to nurture, develop and protect them like family.

Organizational design

From the physical design of office space to the frequency of team meetings, the choices managers make about the structure of the organization reinforce a firm's culture. Capital Group, known for its egalitarian, "no star" culture, goes out of its way to avoid any indicators of status in its office space. Corner offices are only used for conference rooms.[26] All analysts and portfolio managers have offices that are the same size, and if an office is slightly smaller than the norm, an experienced portfolio manager often will offer to move into it. Some investment firms, like the Yale Investments Office, have open floor plans to facilitate organic communication. Others, like many value-oriented managers, create spaces that resemble libraries with quiet, individual offices conducive to reading and reflection.

The frequency and structure of team meetings sets the tone for communication. Wellington Management holds a daily morning meeting across the globe where members of the investment team share insights. Most allocator teams meet less frequently reflecting the slower volume and pace of decisions.

Without proper preparation, team meetings can devolve into a dreaded waste of time. Well-structured meetings have an agenda, purpose, and action steps along the way. They have a prescribed code of conduct and the orchestrator of the meeting keeps the team on point.

CIOs regularly step away from the day-to-day structure of their work by organizing offsite meetings. Changing the setting and regular routine allows the team to think about important strategic topics in a different way.

Project management

With the team and organizational structure in place, managers can turn to getting work done. Tools of project management include prioritization, articulation of tasks, accountability, and updates.

1. Prioritization – focus of effort

Bull Gurfein learned a concept similar to prioritization when in the Marines. When faced with limited resources, priority goes to the most important task at hand. In the military, if you face limited artillery, naval gunfire or airplanes, the resources first go to the unit that is the focus of effort at that time. In investment organizations, the scarce resource is often a CIO's time. If the team as a whole understands the focus of effort, individuals can ease any frustrations that arise when they are sitting outside of that priority for the time being.

2. Articulation – jobs to be done

Jen Prosek defines the roles that her team plays as "Finder, Minder, Binder, Grinder." A *finder* identifies commercial opportunities for the business. *Minders* are great process managers. *Binders* work well on relationships, and *grinders* get the work done. Members of Jen's army may navigate multiple roles or may find they are particularly adept at one. By defining the jobs to be done in this way, Jen manages expectations and deliverables. New employees at Prosek Partners are indoctrinated with the language during the interview process, allowing them to be part of the process of determining where they can add the most value.

3. Accountability – assigning tasks

Diffusion of responsibility is a concept that stuck with me from introductory psychology class in college. In the presence of others, individuals are less likely to take accountability and will assume someone else will get things done. In the workplace, when tasks are assigned to more than one person, the lack of specific accountability may hinder the completion of the project. For example, sending emails to multiple people without specifically naming one to an assignment is a common example of ineffective management.

In the Marines, whenever two people are given a task, one person is always the responsible leader. In companies, however, managers frequently say "Hey everybody, I need you all to get out there and do *x*." As Bull Gurfein says, "When you task everyone, you task no one."

Entrepreneur Dan Schorr learned to manage people at high-functioning, large consumer marketing brands. When he ran a thinly staffed start-up with lots of activity, he needed to manage a laundry list of to-dos efficiently and effectively. Dan used a simple mnemonic of three Ws – Who is doing What and When – to ensure one person was accountable for the completion of every task.

4. Review – status updates

Bull Gurfein regularly consults businesses that struggle with supervision and support. Managers throw out tasks and expect them to get completed. When a few weeks go by and the project isn't finished, managers then engage.

Instead, Bull offers advice on simple ways to better assign tasks to increase the probability of completion. He suggests developing clear plans, priorities, and timelines with milestones. Companies from start-ups to large corporations use the lingo KPIs, or key performance indicators, to define the milestones to achieve objectives.

Scott Kupor similarly defines deliverables and asks his team what they think they will need to meet them.

In his book *Lean Start-Up*,[27] Eric Ries discusses a cycle of building, measuring, and getting feedback to iterate on product development. Patrick O'Shaughnessy uses his vision of learn, build, share, repeat to get at the same idea.

When something goes wrong, good managers perceive problems as learning opportunities. Roz Hewsenian from Helmsley Charitable Trust asks, "What didn't I do for you in terms of direction or instruction, or were you not ready to handle this?" Rather than assigning blame to the team member, she focuses on what she could do better as a manager.

Talent development

No formal training exists for ascending the ranks as an allocator. The CFA charter may teach the fundamental principles of investing and allocation, but the art of investing comes from apprenticeship. The Yale Investments Office has been prolific at churning out future endowment CIOs. Having sat in that classroom for five years, I can assert that the incredible education and training we received was entirely by osmosis.

Professional services firms frequently fall prey to the Peter Principle in their advancement of strong performers. The Peter Principle describes the tendency of most hierarchical organizations to promote employees until they land in a role in which they are not competent to succeed. Greg Fleming saw this on Wall Street, where producers get moved into management positions and lack the tools to manage effectively. The skill set of great leaders is often very different from that of high-performing producers. Managers can navigate around the Peter Principle by incorporating training for those promoted into roles that require a new skill set or by altering their promotion criteria to consider the skill sets required to succeed.

Roz Hewsenian tries not to impose her views, allowing her team space to be creative. She ensures a thorough due diligence process is followed and pays close attention to developing skills. When Roz joins her team at a manager's office, she focuses on her teammates more than the manager. She studies their preparation, the questions they ask, and their responses to the manager's answers. She forms research groups within the team that include a sponsor, a skeptic, and a senior team member to get three sets of informed eyes on every opportunity. This approach allows her to have confidence in the breadth and depth of their work and only step in if she sees a gaping hole in the analysis.

Jen Prosek promotes "Commission for Life" as a mechanism to align the motivation, compensation, and development of her employees. If a team member brings a relationship to the firm that becomes a client, they receive 10% of that client revenue for the life of the client and the life of their employment. By giving a commission for life, she also teaches her army of entrepreneurs how the business operates. If they don't get paid one month, they will notice and may learn about accounts receivable and collections. If pricing changes, they may ask why their commission went up or down. Jen found a compensation scheme that works wonders for her partnership.

Regular feedback is imperative to developing talent. Whether through scheduled 360 reviews or a periodic check-in on objectives, great managers find ways to offer constructive feedback and set goals for development. Allocators often struggle to identify metrics to attach to development, as their profession lacks incremental targets like sales or margins that drive the bottom-line. Nevertheless, creating specific, accountable metrics that tie to impact on the portfolio gives investment leaders a structure through which to regularly review and develop team members.

CIOs themselves also need to develop and learn. Randall Stutman and his team have worked with the heads of many investment organizations to coach effective management and leadership. It can be lonely at the top, so CIOs who engage with peers and coaches stand the best chance of continuing to develop themselves.

Time management

Hiring and developing talent, structuring a team, managing people, and overseeing a portfolio take a tremendous amount of time. In larger organizations, human resources is its own department, dedicated managers lead teams, marketing crafts and tells stories, and operators produce the product. In an institutional pool of capital, the CIO takes on all these roles. A few time management tips may be helpful in figuring out how to get it all done.

Bull Gurfein reminds of the importance of pushing down tasks so that subordinate leaders develop problem-solving skills and resiliency. Leaders too frequently have the desire to save the day. In doing so, they detract from the responsibility of oversight. Bull resists the urge to do things himself and instead asks his team, "Can you figure it out? Tell me what you're going to do to solve it."

Jen Prosek repeats the phrase "Solve, Don't Dwell." She urges her team to put all their energy into solving problems and not stewing when things go wrong. We all have good luck and bad luck moments. Those who shoot the moon recognize good luck and focus on maximizing it without distraction. They also take bad luck moments and find ways to turn them into good luck moments.

Greg Fleming starts his days by thinking about what really matters and what doesn't. He triages what is really important that he has to do to move forward, what great people he has in place to perform where he doesn't need to get involved, and what pieces fall in between.

Chatri Sityodtong creates a four-box matrix across the axis of priority and urgency. Every day, he starts with high-priority, high-urgency tasks, pushes out low-priority, low-urgency, and balances the other two.

Summary

Managing a team of people is an essential, full-time job that ensures that a leader executes on their vision. The tools shared by guests are simple, effective management concepts. Hiring, organizational design, project management, talent development and time management all go into the process of ensuring that the CIO's vision gets implemented.

Thus far, we have covered functional tools employed by CIOs in their role. Now, let's turn to how modern allocators think about and conduct their investment process in Part 2.

To learn more

Podcasts

Capital Allocators: David "Bull" Gurfein – Interdisciplinary Lessons from the Marines (Ep.10)

Books

How to Win Friends and Influence People, Dale Carnegie

Take your pick. There are libraries full of management books. I picked this one because it had the most influence on me.

2

INVESTMENT FRAMEWORKS

Alongside the tools in the toolkit, guests on the show talk in detail about their investing. Part 2 discusses the frameworks modern CIOs employ in managing the money entrusted to them. The sequence from high level to the ground is as follows:

- Governance
- Investment strategy
- Investment process
- Technological innovation

The section closes with a case study on how CIOs handled the uncertainty presented by the Covid-19 pandemic in 2020.

Chapter 6

Governance

"You can't have investment success with a bad governance structure."

– Karl Scheer

A few years ago, a money manager I knew was preparing for its sixth meeting with a major endowment. They had met junior analysts, asset class specialists, and senior staff at the endowment's office and their office, and they had spent a full day visiting portfolio companies together. In this meeting, they were presenting to the CIO for the first time in what they thought would be the final hurdle to begin a valuable relationship. The meeting went well, and the CIO informed them he would make a recommendation to invest at the next board meeting.

A month later, the CIO called the manager to share that the board turned down the recommendation.

That manager was not alone. I sat down with a former CIO of this endowment, which had a reputation for a challenging governance structure. I wasn't sure what that meant, so I asked him what percentage of investment recommendations he brought to the committee were turned down. I was taken aback when he responded, "I'd say 60%." He was at his wit's end. Even when he thought he had buy-in ahead of a meeting, the discussion went awry when egos and infighting among board members took hold.

* * *

CIOs are perceived as sitting at the apex of the food chain of capital. But that is not the whole story.

A consistent theme across all the CIO conversations on the show is the importance of effective governance. CIOs cannot make decisions as if they were autocratic rulers. They too have a client to serve who is the ultimate owner of the capital.

Among different asset owners, family offices may be the simplest to understand. The owners of the capital are family members. The CIO's role is to figure out their objectives and manage the capital accordingly. Easy to explain, but with the complex dynamics of families, among the hardest to implement.

Public pension fund CIOs notoriously manage around bureaucracy. Chris Ailman of CalSTRS has spent 30 years at the helm of public pension funds, despite starting with the premise that "it doesn't take a Harvard grad to figure out that the government running an investment organization is a flawed business model." For Chris to hire an investment manager, his team needs to send out the same government-mandated RFP (Request for Proposal) that the public works staff uses to hire a contractor to oversee construction of a highway.

Endowments have investment committees that report to the trustees of the academic institution. Its members often are knowledgeable and aligned in purpose. Foundations may have a similar set up. Sovereign wealth funds are government-owned pools created to serve their citizens for the long term. While the long duration of capital and consistency of mission is helpful, the potential issues for geopolitical concern and conflict are not.

CIOs and their investment teams do the day-to-day work in setting the agenda and implementing the strategy. When they make recommendations about investment policy, strategy, and manager selection, the board determines whether those recommendations are approved and executed.

The governance structure overseeing these pools of capital has the potential to make or break all the work conducted by CIOs and their teams. Sound governance includes a clear delineation of responsibilities, a highly functioning committee, and incentives aligned with objectives. At the root of all of these is effective communication between the people involved.

Roles and responsibilities

Ben Meng became CIO at CalPERS in January 2019. The $400 billion California pension fund began operations in 1932 to fund and pay pensions to state workers. Over the ensuing 88 years, it has grown to be the largest defined benefit fund in the U.S. and one of the largest pension funds in the world. As CIO, Ben sat at the table at the very top of the global food chain of capital.

Eighteen months later, he resigned. His departure seemed to involve pressure raining down about his potential ties to China, personal ownership of $70,000 of stock in Blackstone Group, and his decision to remove a market hedge in early 2020.[*]

You might assume that a nearly century-old institution with such an important mission would have clear rules in place about political connections, conflicts-of-interest, and short-term investment decisions. But in response to Meng's departure, the CalPERS Board "revealed cracks in philosophy of what power to give staff and what to keep."[28] For what it's worth, Meng wasn't alone. The pension fund's COO and CFO had exited the revolving door of leadership in the last two years as well.

Meng's counterpart in Southern California at CalSTRS, Chris Ailman, says the key with governance is a clear definition of roles and responsibilities. It sounds so simple. Figure out who is doing what and execute. The board and the CIO together decide who is accountable for each step of the investment process and decide who has the authority to make investment decisions.

And yet it is anything but simple.

New CIOs step into their role with a legacy structure that may have contributed to the opening they are brought in to fill. Meredith Jenkins became the first CIO of Trinity Wall Street following the Church's sale of billions of dollars of real estate in 2016. She anticipated walking into the seat with a pile of cash to invest over time, but soon found out that the Church had hired an interim consultant who had rapidly deployed most

---

[*] The timing of the removal of the hedge just before the Covid-19 crisis in March 2020 looked horrible. Six months later with the market fully recovered, Meng's rationale of the undue cost of a hedge over the long term would have sounded a lot better.

of the money. It took Meredith a few years to build the portfolio into the design she had in mind before signing on.

When Ellen Ellison got recruited to be CIO of University of Illinois-Urbana, she took over from a small team in the foundation's offices who had outsourced the investments. She had to deconstruct the ship while it was still in motion. Ellen created a list of 15 agenda items and started with the most difficult one. For six months, she worked on governance and did not touch the portfolio. This included shrinking the size of the investment committee in half, writing new policies for investments, short-term funding, conflict of interests, voting bylaws, and eventually, asset allocation. Only after that groundwork was in place did she turn to reconstructing the investment team and portfolio.

Once a CIO has their bearings, they will find that their authority to make investments can range from full responsibility to none. For Matt Whineray at the New Zealand Super Fund, ownership over all investment decisions is the most fundamental belief. His team makes investment decisions without any required approvals from the board. The Fund's performance is at the top of its peers, in part because of this clear delegation and accountability.

Highly functioning governance processes have a clear delineation of responsibilities. In some organizations like Matt's, the CIO may own the entire asset allocation and manager selection process. At the Getty Trust, the investment office looks to the board to approve the policy portfolio while retaining authority on manager decisions. Jim Williams can move quickly and provide certainty of crossing the finish line with managers. In others, a CIO may retain decisions about manager selection or decisions below a certain size commitment. Lastly, at Helmsley Trust and Carnegie Corporation, the committees retain ultimate authority for all decisions, and yet after thorough discussion almost always defer to the recommendations of the investment office.

In less effective processes the decision-making unit struggles to act consistently. In family offices, the governance process may never get defined. Ron Biscardi of iConnections worked with wealthy families and found that the families struggle with making decisions. Investment issues often are only fourth or fifth on the list of things they spend time talking to each other about. CIOs have a hard time making timely decisions when the thought of investments slips down the agenda of any meeting with the family.

Institutions with more independence and abundant resources tend to rely on internal staff, while those more resource-constrained or with public-facing constituents work with consultants to help navigate governance challenges. Boards lean on consultants as an independent voice with expertise in overseeing effective decision-making. Chris Brockmeyer regularly works with consultants for his clients at the Broadway League. He emphasizes that consultants need to have the trust of all board members to get anything done. Productive consultants sense hot buttons, toe a middle line, and know when to push for new ideas without getting shot down.

Over the last 20 years, many small and mid-sized organizations elected to outsource the entire investment process. OCIO firms, typically founded by a former CIO, bring the benefits of professionalized management, resources and scale that small and mid-sized pools of capital cannot access on their own. OCIOs replace the institution's internal CIO, setting investment policy and strategy, conducting the investment process, reporting to the governance board, and simplifying the complexities of managing assets in a non-investment organization.

Ultimately, the governance board needs to determine how investment decisions get made and who is responsible for them. Then they need to act accordingly, which is where the investment committee itself can get in the way.

Investment committee

"The governance structure is the Achilles heel of this industry. Some of the biggest mistakes we've seen have been when the board panics at the wrong time."

– Meredith Jenkins

Chris Brockmeyer spends his professional life in the boardroom. As the Director of Employee Benefit Funds for the Broadway League, the national trade association for the Broadway theatre industry, Chris serves as an employer-appointed trustee on 11 multi-employer pension funds, seven health funds and four annuity funds, working with 13 boards and four consultants on $7 billion in total assets. Chris prepares for and runs an investment committee meeting every week. He works alongside consultants with everyone from union representatives to owners. Chris described one particularly challenging situation:

> We had a consultant that we had asked to do a private equity search. It took us nearly six months for them to actually start that education process even after we had asked. For some reason, there was resistance, maybe because they weren't experts in the asset class themselves. So once we finally got to the point where we had gotten the education, the RFP process, and the discussions that went on between the consultants, the Union trustees and the employer trustees created an environment where one side wasn't trusting the other side. It might have been that each side felt that the consultant was treating the other side special, so it created something of a toxic environment where the advice that was being given by the consultant was not fully trusted by one or both sides of trustees. Once you get to that point, it's just not possible for a consultant to be effective in giving advice. And so we replaced the consultant and started over.

For each investment committee, the composition of the board, conduct during the meeting, and communication between meetings create the dynamics that determine the quality of decision-making.

1. Composition

The composition of a board is impacted by its chair, size, background of members, and motivation. Steve Galbraith from Kindred Capital believes a CIO needs unbelievable support from the committee chair to be effective. Perhaps none has experienced that more than Scott Malpass. In Scott's 30 years at Notre Dame, he worked with only two investment committee chairs. That continuity allowed Scott the luxury of a deep understanding of the process, familiarity, and efficient dialogue.

Even with a strong committee chair, the size of boards can get unruly. Steve Galbraith serves on boards of a university, a large family office, a public company, a government agency, and two early-stage fintech companies. He found that large committees suffer from a deferral of responsibility and lack a sense of ownership in getting things done. Michael Mauboussin reflected research in Chapter 4, "Decision-Making," that the optimal size of boards is four to six people. When Ellen Ellison reduced the size of her committee in half, it shrunk from 18 to nine and was well on its way to an efficient structure.

The knowledge and experience of board members can fall all over the map. In leading endowments and foundations, the investment committee is composed of sophisticated investment professionals hand-picked by the president of the university or foundation in consultation with the CIO. In others, the board members are teachers and elected officials. Chris Ailman's work requires continuously educating his board, because its members start without sophisticated investment knowledge and turn over regularly with election cycles. Chris Brockmeyer does not work with a single trustee on his 11 boards whose primary job function is investing.

When committees are comprised of investment experts, board members can bring their experience, put the mission of the organization first, and add significant value.

But some board members with investment know-how have ulterior motives for their service. As Steve Galbraith relates, "You'd like to think we're all Mother Theresa and doing things for great reasons. But victory has a thousand fathers and defeat is an orphan." Professional investors with healthy egos may impart their views of how the world works forcefully, as occurred in the university investment office that rejected 60% of the investment team's recommendations. Others may be significant donors to the institution with an agenda. Jim Dunn of Verger Capital offered an example of a board member and donor who was also the CEO of a publicly traded company: "If the CEO gave us a million dollars and we give that money to an activist manager who wants the CEO fired, that's a bad day for me."

Building a productive relationship with the board requires a CIO to work with what they have, establish guidelines for conduct, communicate frequently, and influence decisions about new board members over time.

2. Conduct

When a group of individuals with different experience and motivations come together, navigating the decision-making process is challenging. One of the most important steps a CIO takes is setting expectations for the preparation and conduct of board members upon their arrival to the committee. Charley Ellis sat on Yale's Investment Committee for 16 years and served as the chair for ten. Charley contends that the highly functioning board was not by accident.

> The investment committee is very carefully chosen to be people who, number one, play well with others. They listen well for an understanding of the other person's point of view. The second thing is the depth of homework required. When I was on that committee, I had to set aside an entire day – from eight in the morning until eight at night – studying the documents so that I would be adequately prepared. That's a very unusual characteristic. And then, once a year we had a soup-to-nuts, tear-it-all-apart, look-at-every-single-assumption, does it all really make sense exactly the way it is? Or should we make some minor or mid-sized, or even large changes? That day turned out to be enormously productive. We almost always made no basic changes, but we reaffirmed the strategy, the policies, and the practices that day and understood that was the only day we discussed it.

Few committees have the expectation and commitment of Yale's. Quite the contrary in fact. In his decades of working with clients at AllianceBernstein, Seth Masters found that most boards miss the forest through the trees.

> Most boards end up spending surprisingly little time on the issue of what they are there to achieve and spend a ton of time on little buckets, benchmarks for each of them, and the ones that are doing a little bit worse than benchmarks. It's sort of like someone deciding that they're going to check every newspaper in the world for grammatical and typographical errors instead of understanding whether or not there's fake news.

Managing through the intricacies of the boardroom is an exercise in psychology and human behavior. Chris Ailman describes it as working for a chorus of 12, in which you work with them individually, but you have to listen to the chorus. You can't listen to 12 solos because you are not going to meet their needs. Chris Brockmeyer described the set of skills he draws upon from his prior experience as a labor negotiator: listening, understanding, putting your feet in the shoes of the other side, articulating your difference, and trying to convince the other side that your view is better.

Board struggles come to a head at a key moment in the investment cycle: the inevitable troughs. When human nature takes over, bad decisions happen. Chris Brockmeyer has seen it play out time and again.

> We sell low and buy high. Trustees can get impatient and end up in the trap that so many investors do, firing a manager at their nadir and hiring someone new at their apex.

At the end of the day, CIOs enlist the board in staying the course. That's where communication in between meetings comes into play.

3. Communication

Larry Kochard, now at Makena Capital, was a finance professor at University of Virginia in between the start of his career on Wall Street and serving on the board of Virginia Retirement System and as CIO of Georgetown University and UVIMCO. In his career as an allocator, he never let go of teaching. Larry believes that constantly educating the board is one of the underappreciated aspects of the CIO role. Those who embrace educating, as opposed to viewing it as a waste of time, create more stability for the organization and the investment process.

CIOs regularly reach out to board members before setting foot in the boardroom. By keeping board members apprised of investment activities, tapping into their relationships and knowledge, and teasing out any issues they may have, CIOs gather information before getting surprised in the boardroom. Tom Lenehan from the Wallace Foundation frames it as a process of building trust and generating goodwill with the committee for the times when you really need it by keeping them informed and asking for advice. The process occurs every day, in every meeting, and with every decision.

Different organizations find different approaches most effective in communicating. Sam Sicilia at Hostplus had to learn what recommendations to bring to the board, which not to, and when to engage the board in the process. Karl Scheer at University of Cincinnati found that transparent communication was very important, but he had to balance transparency against accidentally giving away discretion.

Consistent, repeated education between meetings with board members follows the same principle as a leader communicating a vision. By reiterating aspects of the investment philosophy, strategy, and conduct, a CIO improves the quality of meetings and the chances that the board will stay the course in tough times.

Incentives

Jack Meyer stewarded Harvard Management Company from 1990 to 2005, growing the largest endowment in the U.S. from $4.8 billion to $25 billion.[29] During his tenure, Harvard managed most of the money internally, and portfolio managers earned incentives tied to multi-year outperformance. The better the results, the higher the compensation. Harvard's team of money managers accepted significant discounts to comparable roles elsewhere to work for the university. Performance thrived.

But the model lacked the political capital to sustain itself. Year after year, alumnae from the class of 1964 publicly pressured university officials to make investment staff compensation in line with higher education practices.[30] Eventually, Jack and his portfolio managers had enough scrutiny and left. Jon Jacobson founded Highfields Capital, Phill Gross founded Adage Capital, and Jack Meyer founded Convexity Capital. Each received substantial allocations from the endowment that paid them more than what they would have made internally. Harvard's investment program has been in flux ever since.

Investment managers, CIOs, and board members are driven by incentives. Allocators seek alignment with managers, rewarding them for outstanding long-term performance and avoiding situations where they get rich just for showing up.

The structure of CIO compensation leaves a lot to be desired. Despite the attention paid to fees at the manager level, CIOs often do not have economic incentives aligned with their mission. Many family offices pay CIOs a fixed salary and task them to compete with limited financial resources. Public pension funds pay executives steering billions of dollars a government wage.

Changing incentives with these pools of capital is an uphill battle. Ash Williams from the Florida State Board of Administration likens fixing the compensation in the public sector to creating peace in the Middle East. He managed to pull it off in the state of Florida, after six years and between 15 and 20 public meetings working through their advisory council. In the end, it was worth the hassle and a life changer for the state's pension fund.

Endowments and foundations have their own set of compensation issues. The first is political. Donors and professors balk at seeing large compensation paid to investment leaders, as prominently displayed at Harvard. Ashby Monk of Stanford observes that football coaches can make $7 million a year in this country, but paying the same to a CIO is sacrilege.

The second is duration, where the tenure of a CIO is shorter than the duration of the pool of capital they manage. Kip McDaniel from *Institutional Investor* finds that a lot of allocators say they are long-term investors, but their staff compensation is all short term. Even when a CIO has long-term incentives, the measurement period is rarely longer than three years for a pool of capital intended to serve multiple generations of scholars and grant recipients.

The third is comparison, where many CIOs are paid relative to the performance of their peers. Peer compensation is a pernicious practice in the endowment and foundation world. Some CIOs are grouped in peers and compensated relative to a small group of similar-sized institutions, ignoring the unique needs of each institution. The misalignment can lead to perverse behavior. I recall a credit manager sharing that an endowment invested with the caveat that the manager could not accept capital from a list of eight other endowments. By reacting to their incentive, the CIO turned potential collaborators into competitors.

Incentive structures evolve and improve over time. Canadian pension plans are on the right track, designing compensation schemes that reward stability and long-term results. Mario Therrien at CDPQ used the analogy of a hockey player, suggesting he would rather sign a long-term contract with more assurance to get paid over many years than make a lot of money for four years and risk an early end to his career. The Canadian plans have become a model for the future, with less staff turnover and outstanding performance.

Summary

Effective governance may be the most important and least understood driver of investment results for institutions. Clearly delineating roles and responsibilities of the board and investment team, setting up and managing an investment committee, and properly aligning incentives are key attributes of successful governance.

Once the governance structure is in place, CIOs turn to the role they are most known for day-to-day – investing the capital. That process starts with how they view the world. Their investment strategy is the subject of the next chapter.

To learn more

Podcasts

Capital Allocators: Steve Galbraith – In the Boardroom (Ep.48)

White Papers

Best Governance Practices for Investment Committees, Greenwich Roundtable[31]

Principles of Investment Stewardship for Nonprofit Organizations, Commonfund Institute[32]

Chapter 7

Investment Strategy

"To be a good investor, you don't need to have a particular style to your investing, but you do need to have a strong view of what you are doing."

– Ben Inker

The cottage industry of professional institutional allocation with a CIO at the helm is relatively new. When I was an analyst at the Yale endowment in the early 1990s, I may have been the only such person in an allocation role in the entire country. The CIOs on the podcast come from widely diverse professional backgrounds. It is no surprise that this first generation of CIOs have learned the trade on their own. David Swensen's *Pioneering Portfolio Management* is the seminal bible in the field, but reading a book does not compare to lived experience.

CIOs frame their investment activities by articulating a set of beliefs about how the investment world works. Everything that follows is geared towards implementing a disciplined strategy based on those beliefs.

The heart of an investment strategy beats around the purpose for the capital. It influences the investment time horizon, preferences of stakeholders, policy portfolio, and structure of the investment effort.

Purpose

Endowments are tasked with managing intergenerational equity, balancing spending today with preserving the purchasing power of assets for future generations of scholars. Andy Golden refers to his horizon as BLT, or beyond the long term. He strives to not just produce the best possible results over the next 10 years, but also to make sure that at the end of those 10 years, Princeton has a program with unfair advantages for the subsequent 10 years. Their extremely long duration with annual spending along the way leads to an equity orientation and diversification.

Foundations and hospitals have specific missions in their charter. Foundations are established to give back to the world in ways that matter to the original donor. Hospital assets are managed to help those in need. Many are designed to be around for the long term. Other foundations, like Chuck Feeney's Atlantic Philanthropies, are designed to give away all the money in the founder's lifetime.[33]

Australian superannuation funds serve the retirement needs of a young population. At Hostplus, Sam Sicilia oversees a pool of capital that will have inflows for decades before a single Aussie dollar trickles out. His investment philosophy focuses on growing the capital without concern for interim liquidity needs.

Corporate and public pension funds seek to meet the needs of retirees. Their fixed liability streams with finite duration leads to matching liabilities with fixed income assets.

Individuals define their own purpose for the capital they have accumulated. When it comes to investing, Josh Brown of Ritholtz Wealth Management believes that less is more. People who come wanting the bells and whistles of an institutional portfolio within the first conversation get weeded out as prospects. He believes it is for their own benefit.

Time horizon

Institutional pools of capital have a long duration that will outlast any CIO. Career risk is one of the largest motivators in investment decisions, and yet across the board, CIOs express that patience is essential to success.

For Mario Therrien, patience comes with a need for a steady hand in difficult times. He refers to the definition of long-term investing as underperforming for longer than others. Sportswriter Ben Reiter shares a similar lesson when reflecting on the Houston Astros World Series championship in 2017. One of the things that set the Astros apart was patience. They had a stomach for the embarrassment and torture that they went through for years in the basement of the league, and the confidence not to deviate from the plan.[*]

Investors tend to shorten theoretically longer time horizons. While Andy Golden espouses a multi-decade view, he also believes the real time horizon is how long a CIO can go with a large amount of discomfort without changing their path inappropriately. Bill Spitz at Diversified Trust believes that horizon is three years. He finds trustees get antsy after one year of bad results, get really antsy and begin to pull the trigger after two, and take another year to actually do it. Sam Sicilia took a pause at deploying capital at the onset of the pandemic in 2020 when the Australian government blindsided the superannuation industry by offering the population an unanticipated withdrawal right.

Natural habitat

CIOs grow up in the business developing beliefs about how to achieve investment success. David Swensen holds a PhD in economics and anchors his investment philosophy in academic research. Yale has long preferred managers with an equity bias, value orientation, small cap bias, and concentrated portfolio. His protégés learned the trade under his watch, and generally share the same beliefs after observing and contributing to Yale's success.

Ana Marshall grew up outside of the U.S. and started her career immersed in high yield and emerging market debt research. She has a proclivity towards international markets and stresses downside protection.

Overseers of capital increasingly incorporate a holistic integration of beliefs. Historically, governing bodies tasked CIOs with an almost exclusive focus on maximizing investment returns at a given level of risk. More recently, CIOs consider the broad mission of their organization in their investment decisions.

The movement towards sustainable investing by including environmental, social and governance (ESG) factors in the investment analysis is a pronounced change in asset management. CIOs may exclude assets that

---

[*] Admittedly, even Ben was not aware of the embarrassment and torture the Astros would soon go through when investigators disclosed their dubious tactics en route to the championship.

harm the environment, integrate ESG considerations as a lens in decisions, invest thematically in trends that benefit from the movement, or make impact investments intended to address sustainability directly. While overseeing the largest pension fund in the world, Japan's Government Pension Investment Fund (GPIF), Hiro Mizuno realized that its $1.5 trillion in assets is so large that the fund necessarily owns the global portfolio. Rather than focusing his team's efforts on achieving incremental returns above a benchmark, he focused on improving the returns for the global portfolio. Hiro believes that investing in sustainable assets, companies, and markets will promote GPIF's longevity, and he took a series of measures to encourage the entire ecosystem of capital to emphasize ESG in their work.

Policy portfolio

Historically, institutions employed a top-down assessment of asset class characteristics and targets to create policy portfolios. Through quantitative analysis and informed judgement of market conditions, CIOs selected a strategic asset allocation best positioned to meet their objectives. These targets were a significant driver of investment returns and laid the foundation for implementation. Steve Rattner at Willett Advisors contends that in a normal world, the bulk of return comes from beta. Alpha will always be a much smaller component no matter how good you are at picking managers and no matter how good the managers are.

More recently, CIOs have fine-tuned the lens of the policy portfolio. Asset allocation may drive performance in retrospect, but few, if any, CIOs profess skill in forecasting asset class returns. Other than their usefulness as familiar communication language with a board, asset classes leave a lot to be desired as an anchor for portfolios. For one, asset classes can create rigid investment buckets. Roz Hewsenian finds "the box approach" to be a disaster. It forces allocators to compromise standards to fill a box and pass on great investments that don't fit into one.

Traditional asset allocation is also more sensitive to the past than to recent market conditions. Matt Whineray finds that asset classes have a life cycle. As more institutional investors get into an asset class, excess returns decline over time. Paying attention to the changes in asset class attractiveness is an important consideration in future returns. Along these lines, Ben Inker of GMO contends that no investor can intelligently assess any situation before answering the question: "What price am I paying?"

CIOs have innovated on the traditional asset class construct. Moving away from a set of asset class targets builds flexibility into the investment process. Raff Arndt from the Australia Future Fund finds the option value of flexibility is not something that traditional portfolio theory considers. Jim Williams contends that at the end of the day, there are really only two asset classes – owning and lending. Everything else is a permutation. Scott Malpass reduced Notre Dame's asset classes from six to three, leaving just public, private, and opportunistic, distinguished primarily by liquidity. These broader categories allow the investment team to search for the best managers and compare the attractiveness of risk and reward across traditional asset classes.

Seth Alexander at MIT adopted a manager-centric allocation framework in lieu of asset classes. The team searches for exceptional managers independent of their asset class or strategy, and sizes positions based on their conviction in the manager, attractiveness of their underlying holdings, quality of their relationship, liquidity, and diversification characteristics of the strategy to the MIT portfolio. The team carefully measures the resulting risks and sets aggregate limits to maintain sufficient diversification.[34]

Matt Whineray deploys New Zealand's assets through the lens of risk factors. He begins with the creation of a Reference Portfolio, which is a shadow portfolio of easily replicable, low-cost passive investments. The Reference Portfolio moves away from asset classes, emphasizing underlying economic drivers of growth, inflation, liquidity, and agency. It allows the governance board, the Guardians, to estimate expected returns and measure the value of active deviations from the benchmark.

Matt's strategic portfolio is composed of a series of risk budgets that ensure diversification and consistent implementation of active risk. The risk baskets look quite different from common factors in that they define the drivers of return instead of characteristics of underlying investments. The baskets include Asset Selection, Structural, Market Pricing – Arbitrage and Funding, Market Pricing – Broad Markets, and Market Pricing – Real Assets.[35]

As a note of caution, introducing flexibility removes the guidelines that keep decision makers disciplined. "Market timing" is an evil phrase in institutional investing that can be synonymous with flexibility. Within a traditional structure, Jon Hirtle seeks to balance the two through infrequent tilts that can be hugely impactful in avoiding a bubble maybe once every 10 years.

Team structure

Institutional investment offices tend to focus their efforts on hiring external managers. Allocators believe they will generate higher returns by partnering with well-resourced specialists across asset classes, geographies, and strategies than by attempting to compete with them, even after considering the high fee burden involved in doing so.

Organizing the manager selection team takes on different forms. Jim Williams believes that asset class specialists are required to develop deep domain expertise and networks, especially in alternatives. In contrast, Brett Barth from BBR Partners and Kim Lew prefer their teams to be generalists where they can make informed comparisons of risk and reward across the spectrum of opportunities. Donna Snider from Hackensack Meridian Health works with a hybrid model, where senior investment staff are generalists and junior team members are specialists, allowing juniors to learn more, contribute faster, and have a better experience by focusing on one area.

Some large pools of capital are shifting assets towards internal management. Hiring teams to directly manage public and private assets has the benefits of control, liquidity, and cost savings, with the potential drawback of a smaller universe of talent to hire. Kristian Fok from Cbus Superannuation Fund oversees a fund sufficiently large that he couldn't continue to outsource. He needed to do something different to ultimately either increase capacity or replace the return stream, and turned to internal management. Dawn Fitzpatrick at Soros Fund Management bridges that gap by managing internally what they're good at doing themselves and allocating externally with outstanding people in attractive niches.

Ash Williams believes he can find top managers who would prefer living a lower-cost lifestyle near the beaches in Florida than earning an incremental dollar in the bustle of New York City. Steve Rattner refers to their internal direct investing as the special sauce added to an endowment model approach. Steve believes that offering competitive compensation allows him to hire internally while paying less than the 20% carry of an external manager.

Successful internal management may be trickier than it appears. Larry Kochard dabbled with an internal portfolio of public equities in his time at UVIMCO. His team figured out a way of putting on interesting positions directly based on what they learned from managers, but struggled with managing around the positions and knowing when to exit.

Canadian pension funds have led the world in moving assets towards internal management, believing they have the governance, compensation, and talent necessary to succeed. Mario Therrien at CDPQ has watched a shift in internal management over the last two decades to the point where around 90% of the fund's assets are managed internally today. Yet even when the locus of control moves internally, CDPQ sees tremendous value in external manager relationships as their "window to the world."

Summary

CIOs articulate an investment strategy that serves as their guiding light to tackle the investment challenge. This starts with a philosophy and walks through a strategy that sets up the foundation for a CIO to meet their objectives. They then can turn to executing on the strategy in the marketplace, the subject of the next chapter.

To learn more

Podcasts

Capital Allocators: Jon Hirtle – The Pioneer of OCIO (Ep.98)

Capital Allocators: Matt Whineray – Innovation at New Zealand Super Fund (Ep.108)

Books

Pioneering Portfolio Management, David Swensen

Chapter 8
Investment Process

"Having a good process basically sets up your chessboard to deal with more crap. It sets it up in a way that you can take advantage of luck when it comes your way, and that you can defend against the crap when it comes your way."

– Jason Karp

F ollowing the codification of a strategy, the investment leader turns to the process to put the plan into action. Jason Klein refers to this as taking a world view and making it an economically exploitable game plan.

A CIO sets the investment strategy in place and reviews it periodically with the board. The CIO then spends their days implementing the investment strategy, which covers sourcing managers, conducting research, constructing the portfolio, and monitoring investments. Each component is a multi-step process.

Sourcing managers

A well-defined investment philosophy and strategy helps allocators narrow the massive universe of potential investments. According to data gathered by NEPC, active managers oversee approximately 3,850 funds in U.S. equities, 5,100 in international equities, 4,800 in fixed income, 2,300 in balanced strategies, and 8,000 hedge funds. Add roughly 3,200 private equity managers, 5,400 in venture capital, 1,200 in real estate, and 400 in infrastructure, and the investable universe for allocators to consider totals at least 34,250 funds.

The binding constraint on reviewing opportunities is time. An investment office's highest priority is monitoring their existing portfolio of managers. A typical institution might invest in 100 funds across asset classes and meet each of those managers two to four times each year. They also spend a substantial amount of time measuring performance and managing risk. Working with the existing portfolio likely takes up well over half of the team's day.

A simultaneous priority of an investment team is communicating internally and externally. Teams conduct regular internal research meetings and periodic Investment Committee meetings, each of which requires substantial preparation.

With the time left over, investment teams conduct research on new opportunities. This ongoing process includes reading news, strategy pieces, manager letters, and company reports about areas of interest. This work happens before preparing for meetings with manager candidates.

An investment staff is probably left with enough time to see 200–400 new funds each year. In other words, a typical Investment Office reviews no more than 1% of the universe of opportunities potentially available to them. It is six times more difficult for a manager to get a face-to-face meeting with an institutional allocator than a high school senior to gain acceptance at Yale or Harvard.

So how does a CIO direct their team to figure out which managers to consider for their portfolio?

Idea generation starts by narrowing the filter with a set of rules and proceeds to fill the pipeline with referrals from existing managers, ideas from personal and professional networks, shared ideas with peers, and lastly, inbound solicitations.

1. Narrow the filter

By necessity, CIOs use a set of filters to screen out funds less likely to fit in their portfolio. Raff Arndt, who oversees the A$160 billion ($105 billion) Australia Future Fund, does not spend time with funds in which he can't deploy hundreds of millions of dollars. In contrast, Ellen Ellison from the $3 billion University of Illinois Foundation has a penchant for managers that are a good bit smaller, but not too small. She tends to avoid big funds and searches for those that fit a sweet spot between big enough for comfort and small enough to take advantage of less efficient areas of the markets. Other common screens might include ownership structure, breadth of product offering, tenure of organization, length of track record, and assets under management.

These rules of thumb will eliminate some outstanding managers from consideration, but errors of omission are less of a concern for CIOs. Anne Martin of Wesleyan believes, "you don't have to do every good deal, just every deal that you do has to be good." Similarly, Brett Barth is comfortable with not making an investment he wishes he had, but is really uncomfortable with hiring a manager he wishes he hadn't.

2. Existing portfolio

Most CIOs find the preponderance of their new investment opportunities from referrals by managers in their portfolio. Portfolio managers share an investment philosophy with the CIO, fit into the strategy, are selected for skill, and have a vested interest in the CIO's success. Scott Malpass views his managers as the smartest people he knows in the markets. Otherwise, he would not invest with them.

Scott regularly asks managers about the best talent in their space or network. He also turns to managers for specific on-the-ground insights when considering a new manager for the portfolio.

3. Internal network

CIOs also leverage the personal and professional contacts of team members and the board to identify and screen new managers. Roz Hewsenian ensures that everyone on the team is part of this process. She believes that young people surface differentiated findings because they are less burdened with the bias that comes with experience.

Some CIOs work with external consultants to broaden their network of opportunities. A CIO may hire a consultant to outsource idea generation, leverage the consultant's due diligence resources, serve as a sounding board, or check-the-box in due diligence. The degree of integration with the consultant is related to the resources of the CIO – those with more resources of their own tend to rely on outside advisors less.

4. Peers

Institutional allocators travel in packs. Each investment team takes pride in finding their own ideas, but most find a few trusted peers with whom they share ideas and broaden their intimate networks.

5. Inbound

A harsh reality for many managers is that almost no relationships with allocators arise from inbound cold calls. Unless a manager has found their way in the door through another manager in the portfolio, the internal network of the team, or their peers, it can be exceedingly difficult to get the attention of an investment team.

Target characteristics

Allocators dread the question inevitably served up when they speak on a panel in front of an audience of hungry managers: what do you look for in managers?

Distilling a complex task into a simple framework is insufficient to describe the methodical process allocators practice every day to fill their portfolios. But if you stay around the industry long enough, you'll eventually hear a panel espouse a range of alliterative phrases that attempt to describe rules of thumb for manager selection.

3 As: Approach, Advantage, and Alignment

3 Ps: People, Process, and Performance

5 Ts: Talent, Trendy, Tracking Error, Tails, and Tolls

Each of these simplifications has some merit. They speak to the importance of people, competitive advantage, and results. I once joined the fray at an industry conference with my own version of alphabet soup. "Location, location, location" is a commonly used cliché to describe the three most important characteristics of a real estate investment. I responded with a variation on the theme, that the three most important aspects of hiring a money manager are the 3 Cs: character, character, and character.

Getting away from forced alliteration, CIOs focus on character, alignment of interests, competitive advantage, and terms.

1. Character

Every CIO speaks to the quality of people as tantamount in their choice of partners. Guests shared some of their favorite aphorisms describing why.

> "People of great character never lose it. People who do not have great character never get it."
>
> — *Charley Ellis*

> "Past performance is not necessarily indicative of future results, except when it comes to character."
>
> — *Jon Harris*

> "There's no such thing as a good deal with a bad person."
>
> — *Brett Barth, Tom Russo, and Matt Botein*

Assessing good character is highly subjective. Judgment, humility, trustworthiness, and ethics are commonly cited innate characteristics. Other sought-after components include competitiveness, pedigree, curiosity, motivation, self-awareness, and even-temperament.

CIOs expand their character assessment from the individual leader to the culture of the organization. Randall Stutman defines culture as the set of learned behavioral norms in the firm. Allocators spend time with the team surrounding the leader to look for a cohesive, consistent culture.

2. Alignment

The phrase "alignment of interests" is never far from a CIO's lips. Compensation arrangements, appropriate assets under management, and transparency all give comfort that a manager will act in a way that serves investors.

Charley Ellis distinguishes between the business of asset management and the profession of investing. The business is about growing fees and revenues, whereas the profession is about generating excess returns. Allocators prefer investing with those who practice the profession and monitor the inherent tension between the two. Managers need a healthy business to pursue the profession of investing effectively, but when economic incentives swing the pendulum too far away from the profession, results can suffer.

Determining the appropriate asset size for a strategy is more an art than a science. Managers pursuing strategies that require significant infrastructure may need to be large to compete effectively. Managers in strategies that benefit from flexibility may find that growth in assets shrinks their opportunity set.

The degree of transparency is another important issue. Allocators want to stay on top of the evolving organization they back, the strategy pursued, and the risk exposure they hold in ever-changing markets. The more open and frank the lines of communication, the more an allocator gains comfort with the relationship.

3. Competitive advantage

Successful investing requires capturing an elusive "edge." Michael Mauboussin uses the acronym "BAIT" to describe the competitive advantage a manager may have, and which allocators seek to identify.[*]

B: Behavioral – managing around behavioral biases, including overconfidence, confirmation bias, anchoring, loss aversion and recency bias.

A: Analytical – processing the same information better than other investors, including raw intellectual horsepower or skill in portfolio construction.

I: Informational – possessing better information than other participants, such as computational power over short time horizons.

T: Technical – identifying non-fundamental reasons why others act, often arising from principal-agent issues and liquidity needs and having access to capital to take advantage of dislocations.

---

[*] Michael focuses on public equity markets, but his framework is broadly applicable across asset classes.

In "Investment Lessons" in Part 3, guests share their take on what constitutes an investment edge.

4. Terms

Deal terms factor in as well. Allocators prefer fees tied to incentives, capital duration consistent with the strategy, and long-term oriented investors alongside them.

Manager fees are a constant source of scrutiny. Boards cannot know net performance, but they see the fees they pay in advance. The end owners of capital can only "eat" net returns. History has not shined brightly on high fees across the industry. Peter Kraus from Aperture Investors notes that allocators choose from a pool of managers whose fee structure and motivation is set up to grow assets, which undermines the performance that the allocator is trying to achieve.

Larry Kochard tries to figure out ways to reduce fees without sacrificing quality. But many CIOs express that they are happy to pay for outstanding performance.

> "I'm willing to pay almost any level of fees if I believe the net performance is going to be superior."
>
> — *Steve Rattner*

> "I wake up every morning saying a prayer that I'm going to pay the most in fees this year that I've ever paid."
>
> — *Jon Harris*

> "People don't mind paying fees as long as they are structured the right way. If you pay peanuts, you get monkeys."
>
> — *Rahul Moodgal*

> "You're kidding yourself if you think you can get the combination of extraordinary performance and very low fees. When you find true talent, you have to pay them."
>
> — *André Perold*

Beyond fees, allocators study the litany of terms in legal documents to qualify how managers think about and treat their investors. Christie Hamilton from Dallas Children's Health finds that it takes work to read all the documents, because "it's usually the 10th paragraph on the 30th page that you should question." Jon Harris wonders whether private equity investors are *limited* partners or limited *partners*. He highlights a litany of terms for investors to scrutinize in a market that has shifted negotiating power towards managers.[36]

Due diligence

Conducting research on a new investment opportunity includes a series of face-to-face meetings, behind-the-scenes research, and an investment recommendation. Allocators evaluate the attractiveness, consistency, and repeatability of the desired characteristics of managers and their investment process. With the exception of capacity-constrained situations, allocators typically get to know a manager over years before committing capital. Bill Spitz compares the manager selection process to dating, saying "you're better off not making a decision on the first try."

1. Meetings

The first few meetings focus on the background of the people and their story, often told in different settings and by different people to test consistency. When visiting a manager's office, Tim McCusker from NEPC focuses on seeing how a team engages with one another. He looks to see the dynamics of the room, the hierarchy of command, and the quality of exchange. Anne Martin takes managers away from the office to learn more about them. She figures that if she doesn't want to go to dinner with someone, she shouldn't invest. She wants to know that her relationship with the manager can withstand the terrible times in the trenches together.

Later meetings dive into the investment process, portfolio construction, and underlying investments. Scott Wilson and his team at Washington University in St. Louis re-underwrites a manager's investments, conducting independent security analysis to confirm the attractiveness of investment ideas.

2. Research

Allocators complement the set of interactions with an independent review. They read the materials provided by the manager, confirm statements through research of publicly available information, meet with competitors, and conduct exhaustive reference checks. Allocators often employ a due diligence checklist to ensure all the work gets completed.

And lest we forget, allocators will inevitably study past performance. Some will use past performance as an indicator of future performance. More astute allocators will use the track record to learn more about the manager's past behavior in good times and bad. Past performance is not an indicator of future returns, but temperament tends to persist over time.

CIOs gather all the diligence with their team and weigh the opportunity against risk. Anne Martin is comfortable moving away from the crowd, but wants to know what she sees that others do not. If she likes a manager and no other great investors are alongside her, then she goes back to figure out what she thinks that nobody else does. She may be right, but she wants to triple check her work.

Steve Rattner contends that after all the work, investing in managers is ultimately a judgment call. He looks at the person to sense if they have the drive and the determination to be great.

3. Recommendation

Allocators encapsulate their research in a written investment recommendation presented to the decision-making body. These memoranda cover every aspect of the manager – background, team, opportunity, idea generation, research, decision-making, portfolio construction, risk management, performance, and operations.

Much in the same way traders keep a journal to understand their thought process in real-time, thoughtful allocators include a concise investment thesis and risks they identify in advance. An effective thesis is based on disprovable evidence rather than a statement of fact, so that allocators can regularly review the thesis without being anchored to recent performance. I used to tell my team that a thesis tied to a manager's intelligence does not help the investment process unless we periodically tested their IQ score with the intention of redeeming when we discovered a deterioration. A better thesis might involve one of the BAITs, such as a private equity firm's ability to improve profit margins of an acquired business through operational excellence.

Portfolio construction

CIOs determine the size of individual positions by taking into consideration policy asset allocation targets, conviction in the manager, liquidity profile, and risk. They look through manager line items to the underlying assets held by the manager when considering the proper position size in the portfolio.

One tricky aspect of portfolio construction is the necessity to blend static, nominal capital commitments to private funds with a dynamic pool of assets whose value fluctuates based on market conditions. Allocators attempt to model the expected timing of contributions and distributions across private investments to estimate the appropriate position size. Still, the Global Financial Crisis left many institutions with higher commitments to private assets than they intended after their asset corpus shrunk with the collapse of public markets in 2008.

Monitoring

Investment organizations are dynamic. Allocators regularly review their investment thesis and risks to re-underwrite managers in their portfolio. The process focuses on change relative to expectations in the product and performance.

1. Product – firm and fund

Investment firms evolve over time. Bill Spitz believes that manager turnover occurs due to qualitative changes in strategy, style, personnel, or motivation.

Nascent firms have growing pains. Randall Stutman sees expertise limited to investment. Managers really don't know how to create an organization, team culture, build people, and most importantly, engage the organization in a way that is a positive contributor to their investment process.

When firms successfully work through these early stages and generate strong returns, allocators closely monitor how the manager responds. Good results give the manager an opportunity to grow. Some managers stay disciplined; others wave in money when it is available.

Managers have an economic incentive to grow assets under management, introducing a set of issues for investors. Josh Wolfe at Lux Capital draws a parallel with nature – slime mold to be specific. He notes that when resources are abundant, people feel the freedom to spread out and try lots of experiments. Unfettered asset growth can infringe on the integrity of the existing strategy, and inbound interest can enable a manager to expand its product offering. Some asset growth and new offerings add value to the existing fund and strengthen the organization. Too much can create distractions and add complexity in running the business.

Allocators are sensitive to a manager's need to balance the investment aphorism "size is the enemy of performance" with the business mantra "grow or die." Andy Golden sees the benefits of a manager sticking to its knitting, but recognizes that the world changes and managers have to evolve. The question he poses is whether the manager is evolving in a way that inspires confidence.

From a personal perspective, good times reveal hubris in some managers and humility in others. Allocators prefer the latter. Red flags arise when allocators sense overconfidence and greed. Richard Lawrence of Overlook Investments believes that greedy business philosophies are the enemies of performance more than size. Peter Kraus finds that when ego-driven investors are successful, they tend to undermine their self-awareness. They believe too much in themselves and become blind to seeing the truth clearly. Kip McDaniel finds that when people amass a certain amount of wealth, they control almost every aspect of their lives and fight the few instances when it is not the case.

Managing through the down times can be a catalyst for change as well. Managers may drift away from a cyclical strategy that hasn't been working, creating the prospect of getting whipsawed. Underperformance can be reflexive for a manager, leading to asset withdrawals and pressure on the business. The smaller the organization, the more outflows cause fragility. Even allocators who perceive short-term performance challenges as future opportunities are sensitive to the actions of other investors jeopardizing the integrity of the firm. Adam Blitz has found that managers can turn losers into permanent losses when they have a weak investor base that gets jittery in a period of bad performance. Redemptions during these periods force the manager to sell at the worst time.

Tough times also unearth conflicts among partners or key contributors. Many investment organizations are unstable and rely on the character of a few to hold the fabric together. When friction leads to a separation, allocators scrutinize what is left afterwards. Exit interviews of departing employees can be a leading indicator of long-standing organizational issues. Some firms prevent former employees from saying anything of value. Others are supportive of those moving on to different opportunities. These interviews are put in context. Departing team members have their own agenda, and firms have a reputation and business to protect. Although allocators may have to take what they hear with a grain of salt, conducting conversations with former employees helps paint an insider's picture of the organization in which they entrusted their capital.

A manager who stays calm better handles inevitable challenges that arise in the business. Resilience and resolve are essential traits in prolonged success. If the business weathers a storm and the manager demonstrates a steady hand, allocators are emboldened to stay the course.

2. Performance

Astute CIOs use periods of excessively good and bad performance to calibrate expectations. Strong performance can be an impetus for undesired change and weak performance can test organizational stability and personal temperament.

Human behavior leads to performance chasing from both managers and allocators. An investment memo articulates expected risks to the strategy, and yet CIOs may still struggle when reviewing these risks. Inevitably, some risks come to pass and coincide with periods of weak performance. Does the risk therefore render the manager unfit to continue in the portfolio? Or is the risk a natural part of expectations on a bumpy path to investment success?

Michael Mauboussin reflects on a common situation:

> So you give your money to a money manager, and the results have not been good. Either actual skill didn't reveal itself or they've lost their marbles. Part of the assessment is to say,

"Can we constantly reassess the process?", "Does the analytical backbone continue to be sound?", "Is that organization making sure they are managing and mitigating behavioral things?" and "Are they dealing with agency issues appropriately?"

Icing on the cake

The core engine that drives a CIO's performance is the collection of managers that survive the rigorous investment process. It's the cake, if you will. That cake takes many years to bake from scratch, and the mix of ingredients changes slowly.

CIOs take pride in forming long-duration partnerships with their managers. The benefits of long-term relationships include deeper mutual understanding of the mission and value proposition, the delivery of stable capital to pursue long-term investing, and a shared understanding of expectations.

Infrequent changes to the manager roster leave CIOs with bandwidth to devote to other value-added investment activities, or the icing on the cake. These activities include rebalancing, overlays, co-investments, low-cost substitutes, internal management, and relationship management.

1. Rebalancing

When volatility moves the asset allocation away from targets, investors can add incremental returns through the repeated, disciplined practice of rebalancing assets to targets.[37] Michael Cembalest from J.P. Morgan has seen that investment committees for institutional clients are religious about rebalancing. As asset prices go up, they rebalance back to normal, and they add risk when markets go down.

Rebalancing typically occurs across U.S. equities, international equities, fixed income, and cash. Allocators get more granular and rebalance within asset classes, considering capitalization, geography, and other risk factors. The proliferation of low-cost ETFs provides CIOs readily available instruments to rebalance to target portfolios without needing to change manager allocations. Richard Lawrence points out that rebalancing is perfect because it is a completely unemotional event.

2. Overlays

The selection of active managers occurs bottom-up. Allocators spend a lot of time and effort aggregating the exposures of each individual manager to assess risk in the overall portfolio. In addition to rebalancing when markets move positions away from desired targets, CIOs may use overlay strategies to alter the composition of the portfolio. Matt Whineray employs a strategic tilting portfolio to emphasize long-term mean reversion in the risk budget.

Overlay strategies typically reduce risk at perceived extremes in market conditions. Timing peaks perfectly is impossible, but some allocators act when they sense markets are fraught with risk. These actions start with an increase in cash balances, where the only cost is opportunity cost. Allocators then tweak the position sizing or composition of the manager roster, favoring those with lower risk profiles or adding a manager specializing in tail risk protection. Additionally, CIOs create direct programs to hedge downside tails through put options, futures, or swaps on equity or fixed income indexes.

3. Co-investments

CIOs take baby steps towards direct investing through co-investments with managers in their portfolio. The rationale for incorporating co-investments varies across allocators. Roz Hewsenian uses co-investments to increase private equity exposure at lower cost. Jim Williams believes co-investments make up their best performing investments across asset classes. Scott Wilson sees co-investments as the sourcing filter to build a concentrated portfolio.

Co-investment processes to source, screen, and vet the opportunities are designed to match the intent of the program. Roz reviews private equity co-investments through the lens of manager selection, identifying the greatest strengths of each manager across size, sector, and geography and co-investing whenever an opportunity arises that is consistent with those strengths. Jim wants to know that the general partner has real skin in the game and ensures the manager is putting personal capital into the co-investment. Scott underwrites each individual co-investment opportunity.

Co-investing is not for everyone. Daniel Adamson, of Wafra and Capital Constellation, finds that asset owners have eyes that are bigger than their stomachs. Most can't move quickly enough to get to a decision in time-sensitive deals.

4. Low-cost manager substitutes

Allocators are cognizant of the high cost of active management services. Those with large balance sheets negotiate economic terms with managers in situations where they hold bargaining power.

Many also search the markets for opportunities to achieve similar returns to managers at a discount. In my time at Yale, I followed the closed-end fund market in the U.S. and investment trust market in the U.K. to search for talented managers overseeing listed funds trading at discounts to net asset value. More recently, some family offices and institutions have created programs to replicate public manager portfolios by buying stocks listed in 13F regulatory filings in the U.S. or purchasing publicly listed asset managers. These programs raise intriguing questions about the nature of the relationship between allocator and manager, and about what constitutes fee-worthy, value-added services.

5. Internal management

The choice to hire external managers need not consume the entire portfolio. Some institutions have dedicated internal resources to the most efficient areas of the market, where they may buy low-cost index funds or manage passive strategies internally. Internal management allows more control and opportunities to conduct capital market activities that inform the manager selection process. Ash Williams takes a hybrid approach in which members of his team manage passive and quantitative equity strategies, while others search for outstanding external managers.

6. Relationship management

Entering a new investment is fun and exciting. CIOs have the privilege of calling the manager to let them know they are ready to get married for the long term. The honeymoon period is about to begin.

Exiting a relationship is far less enjoyable. Almost all these marriages eventually come to an end. In the best case, a manager may retire and both sides blissfully waltz into the sunset. Only a tad of residual angst remains for the allocator, who needs to find a replacement after enabling the manager's retirement by paying fees over the term of the successful partnership.

More often, CIOs change their mind. They may have a negative view of future prospects or may conclude they made a mistake. In private markets, decisions typically come to a head when a manager seeks to raise capital for a successor fund. In public markets, it can happen at any time.

Irrespective of the cause, CIOs carefully consider the message they deliver when entering and exiting manager relationships. Setting a proper tone at the onset and conducting themselves with empathy upon departure can have ripple effects on how they and their organization are perceived in the marketplace. While less direct an impact than the other icing on the cake, a CIO's conduct can positively or negatively affect their ability to gain access to desired opportunities down the road.

Summary

A methodical investment process across sourcing managers, conducting due diligence, constructing portfolios, monitoring, and adding incremental value allows a CIO to implement on their strategy.

Many of the skills required in the process are qualitative. Each of the tools in the toolkit in Part 1 is an example.

But in a world rapidly embracing technology, CIOs also need to consider how quantitative tools can help improve their investing results, which is the subject of the next chapter.

To learn more

Podcasts

Capital Allocators: Scott Malpass – The Fighting Irish's Twelfth Man (Ep.25)

Capital Allocators: Kim Lew – The Carnegie Way (Ep.52)

Capital Allocators: Andrew Golden – Princeton University's Chief Investing Tiger (Ep.13)

Every CIO on the show adds value thinking about the investment process. I could not pick among them, so I didn't. Scott, Kim and Andy's conversations are the listeners' picks – the most downloaded shows among the CIO interviews.

Chapter 9
Technological Innovation

"What gets measured gets managed."

– Jenny Heller

Financial history repeatedly reminds us that an over-reliance on models can lead to trouble. Seth Masters points out that risk models assume the world will stay the same as in the recent past, whereas so-called hundred-year floods occur every decade. CIOs recognize the fallibility of the past in predicting the future and focus decisions on qualitative factors accordingly.

That said, technological innovation across industries is accelerating change at an unprecedented rate. Sophisticated quantitative analysis to improve allocator outcomes is still in the early innings. CIOs use some long-standing tools to look at past markets in calibrating base rates and expectations in asset allocation, risk management, and performance assessment. Financial technology companies are pushing the envelope to help public equity managers improve. Their work may be a sign of things to come.

Asset allocation

The math of asset allocation draws on Modern Portfolio Theory, developed by Harry Markowitz in 1952. Taking inputs of expected return, standard deviation, and correlation across asset classes, Markowitz's model uses mean-variance optimization to create an efficient frontier. Along the frontier, investors can choose the asset mix that offers the highest return per unit of risk.

While elegant in principle, Modern Portfolio Theory is based on assumptions that do not hold in the real world. The model requires normally distributed returns and accurate, stable expectations of return and risk. It envisions a trade-off of two asset classes, lacking a consideration of the illiquid assets that appear in institutional portfolios today.

CIOs also study past events to understand what might happen to their portfolio in future periods of market turmoil. They conduct Monte Carlo simulations to consider the probability of falling short of long-term investment objectives, such as purchasing power for a perpetual pool of capital or liability matching for a pension fund. Scenario analysis and stress tests also help assess possible short-term losses.

Risk measurement

Measuring risk is a backward-looking assessment of the composition of the portfolio. In addition to portfolio-level metrics, CIOs assess risk manager-by-manager, looking both at return streams and underlying security characteristics.

Returns-based analysis can unearth hidden factor bets. Allocators identify statistical correlations with risk factors by regressing a manager's return stream to historical returns of a range of asset classes. These calculations at times return spurious correlations, like an unexplainable correlation with an obscure foreign currency. Other times what appears spurious may spur exploration, such as correlation to the Nigerian naira, a currency tied to a significant oil-exporting nation.

Allocators also aggregate risk exposures by manager to calculate market risk across factors. Typical risk exposures include asset class, geography, size, sector, style (value/growth), quality, macroeconomic (interest rates, currency), ownership, duration, liquidity, and ESG. Measuring risk at a snapshot in time and regularly repeating the exercise allows allocators to calibrate where and to what degree unintended biases lurk in the portfolio.

Risk management

Measuring risk is a prerequisite for managing risk. The former is an inexact science. The latter is an art. The goal of risk management is to achieve the maximum return with a given level of risk, or to achieve the minimum level of risk given a targeted rate of return.

CIOs achieve this by striving to hold a portfolio that takes on prudent risks in accordance with both their long-term return goals and short-term institutional temperament to stay the course through tumultuous markets. In Part 3, guests offer their perspectives on managing volatility to survive the bumpy path to investment success.

Risk management is not a cure-all to eliminate downside risk. Without risk, there is no return. It is an attempt to consider a probability distribution of potential outcomes. When Mark Baumgartner thinks about risk, he looks carefully at the concentration, leverage, and liquidity of each manager to evaluate the potential for negative outcomes.

However, the biggest risk to portfolios is an unforeseen tail event. As the late Peter L. Bernstein said, "risk means you don't know what will happen." Financial setbacks over my career, which started a few years after the crash in 1987, included the dot.com bubble in 2000, the Global Financial Crisis in 2008, the coronavirus pandemic in 2020, and many smaller sell-offs along the way. Each of these were shocks to the system. Doctors referred to SARS-CoV-2 as a "novel" coronavirus. The sudden stop to economies around the world was indeed novel – it had never happened before.

Each tail event reminds CIOs of the problems of assumptions that underpin models. The dot.com bubble followed an assumption that the new technology of the internet would forever change how business was conducted and valued, a premise priced into the markets about a decade early. The financial crisis resulted, in part, from excessive leverage in the mortgage sector based on the underlying assumption that real estate prices across the U.S. would never fall simultaneously. The pandemic that shook markets in 2020 resulted from an unforeseen health crisis.

Financial history reminds us that CIOs cannot circumvent every pothole in the road. Risk management instead applies informed judgement to risk measures to best position the portfolio to meet long-term objectives.

Performance assessment

The tools of performance measurement differ depending on the intent of the exercise. CIOs assess their own performance, private market managers, and public market managers across a range of metrics to evaluate success.

1. CIOs

Ultimately, CIOs are accountable for their results. Performance is measured against benchmarks for the policy portfolio, asset classes, and individual managers. The results are reported to governance boards every quarter, even though the pool of capital is invested with a much longer duration in mind.

Performance assessment considers a range of measurements. At the total portfolio level, a blended, customized benchmark of indexes assesses the return of the policy portfolio, allocation shifts away from policy, and implementation within asset classes. The success of active management within asset classes includes market indexes and manager peer groups to determine the absolute and relative value-added of manager selection. Some CIOs are also measured and compensated against a close group of peer institutions. This incentive structure at times creates the pernicious practice of turning collaborators into competitors.

2. Private market managers

Statistical analysis of private market managers is in the nascent stages. Private market managers typically make fewer investments and hold positions for longer than public market managers, resulting in a thin data set.

Investment performance in private strategies is also fuzzy. Managers control fund flows in a drawdown structure, so apples-to-apples time-weighted returns are not relevant. Instead, managers report dollar-weighted returns or IRRs, which are subject to trickery. IRRs are juiced by credit lines and skewed from early one-off events. The metric also does not consider the opportunity cost of uncalled capital commitments.

Allocators look across a range of return metrics and cash-on-cash multiples to determine private market manager performance. Chris Douvos refers to his KPI as "moolah in da coolah." Allocators use metrics with the acronyms TVPI (total value to paid-in capital), DVPI (distributed value to paid-in capital), and RVPI (residual value to paid-in capital) to measure manager success. Any amounts not yet distributed in the calculation of TVPI and RVPI are subject to fair value manipulation, particularly in situations when managers are preparing to raise capital for a successor fund.

Deeper analysis of private funds ties results to the people responsible for individual investments and the levers of return. Allocators carefully track which principals led each investment, as private market owners can significantly impact outcomes. Private equity allocators dissect whether financial leverage or operating improvements drove returns and compare those changes to public market peers during the holding period.

The backward-looking nature of statistical analysis tends to be a lagging indicator of private asset performance. Chris suggests inverting the process by calculating the future exit required of each investment in the portfolio and checking that outcome against the company's progress. In the venture capital world, an allocator might ask how big a company needs to be to return half of the fund. In buyouts, the allocator might study how portfolio companies are tracking operationally to each return 20% or 30% of the fund.

3. Public market managers

Public markets, in contrast, offer a wealth of data. Allocators calculate a series of statistics to assess manager skill and behavior. "Past performance is not an indication of future returns" is emblazoned across every investment manager presentation and legal document. Nevertheless, human nature leads investors to follow strong short-term performance with their allocations. Allocators will never be rewarded for the past success of a manager.

Thoughtful CIOs scrutinize a track record and use creative analytics to focus on the strengths and weaknesses of the manager. Allocators weigh an array of statistics to measure returns relative to a benchmark, including time-weighted and dollar-weighted returns, Sharpe ratio (return per unit of risk, measured by standard deviation of returns), Sortino ratio (return per unit of downside risk), exposure-adjusted returns, and peer analysis.

Each of these can be fine-tuned depending on the question a CIO seeks to answer. Comparing time-weighted and dollar-weighted returns can inform a CIO about the quality of the investor base and the manager's messaging. Exposure-adjusted returns scrutinize alpha relative to alternatives in the market, and peer groups tease out whether the investment team made a good choice.

Allocators also use past performance to ask questions about behavior. Questions starting with "What happened when …", "What did you do when …", and "Why did you take that action" around notable stretches of atypically strong or weak performance can shed light on how a manager may respond to similar periods in the future.

Leading edge of data analytics

A small coterie of financial technology start-ups are putting tools to decompose and improve performance in the hands of allocators and managers. These companies are spin-outs of well-resourced managers, and CIOs can consider this the next frontier of data analysis. We are still in the early innings of adoption of sophisticated technology in the allocator game. These tools help in the assessment of manager skill, style drift, and portfolio manager development.

1. Analyzing manager skill

The increasing availability of granular data can help allocators investigate underlying drivers of return to learn about manager skill. Basil Qunibi is a former hedge fund allocator who created Novus Partners to help the world's top investors generate higher returns. Novus provides tools to analyze the attributes of public equity manager skill. Basil created a framework that broke down the five degrees of freedom managers deploy in plying their trade:

1. Exposure – the degree and type of market exposure.

2. Capital allocation – the instruments and sectors the positions represent.

3. Security selection – the stocks picked compared to other alternatives.

4. Position sizing – the success in relative sizing of positions within the portfolio.

5. Tactical trading – the entry and exit of positions.

Studying each of these return drivers separately, Novus uses a set of statistical analyses to pin down the source and persistence of a manager's past results. Allocators review a manager's batting average (% of successful positions) and slugging percentage (magnitude of positions that generate positive returns vs. negative returns). Each of these calculations are conducted across geography, market cap, sector, liquidity, and concentration.

A second block of analysis studies a manager's portfolio in the context of its competitors to inform about drawdown risk due to liquidity shocks. Novus researches the 4Cs: crowdedness, conviction, concentration, and consensus.

2. Projecting style drift

Understanding the drivers of manager performance alerts allocators to potential issues when a manager grows. If a manager doubles its AUM, they necessarily change the character of the portfolio across the number of positions, market capitalization, or liquidity. If the manager maintains the same number of positions and wants to play in the same market cap space, they will be forced to reduce the liquidity of the portfolio. In his many years analyzing the data, Basil has yet to see a manager that experienced greater than 60% liquidity deterioration survive in the long term.

If the manager chooses to maintain liquidity and hold the same number of positions, they will have to invest in larger market cap names. This practice is condemned by allocators as style drift. Lastly, if they maintain liquidity and the investable universe, the manager will be forced to diversify into more names.

The analytics that decompose a manager's skill help inform allocators about risks in the future as changes to the portfolio and business occur. If the preponderance of a manager's outperformance occurred in small cap positions, a decision to move into mid-cap names might not be a good one. A consumer stock specialist departing the firm may be a problem if the consumer sector was the leading driver of past performance.

Statistical analysis of past performance has its limitations. Full transparency of trading in a fund with reasonable turnover over a few years is required to draw statistically significant conclusions. Monthly performance attribution and quarterly 13F filings are not sufficient. Even then, the past is not the future and rigorous statistical work is only one input that can assist the manager assessment process. Despite these flaws, great analytical work helps allocators ask better questions and potentially get one step ahead of the future.

3. Portfolio manager development

Modern data analytics help managers recognize and improve their portfolio management prowess. Large platform hedge funds with frequent trading have the data and resources to extract elusive alpha. Matthew Granade at Point72 sees advantages to economies of scale in their ability to invest in risk systems, trading systems, data systems, research and trading.

Jordi Visser at Weiss Multi-Strategy Advisers relates that if he asked someone in the past why they made or lost money, they told him a story. Armed with data, he can learn the real story and ask questions about the manager's actions. He no longer pays attention to stories without supporting data.

Jordi believes you must show managers their biases for them to improve. He compares the practice to watching a baseball game on television. Statisticians project a box that shows a hitter's batting average on pitches above and below their waist. If they are a better low-ball hitter, can access the data, and restrain from swinging at pitches up in the strike zone, their batting average will improve.

Clare Flynn Levy and Cameron Hight were frustrated former hedge fund managers at smaller shops who felt they did not have the requisite tools to improve their own skills. They set aside managing money to create software companies that would help portfolio managers.

Clare Flynn Levy founded Essentia Analytics with a mission to use technology and data to improve investment performance. Essentia studies trades through the lens of behavioral finance, seeking to identify a manager's biases and inform the manager when they might be making a mistake. The assessment includes entering, adding and trimming, and exiting trades. Nudges assist managers in moving away from their instinctive, reptilian brain – Daniel Kahneman's System 1 thinking – and towards their contemplative part of the brain – System 2.

There is one aspect of Essentia that needs mentioning. Charley Ellis, the same outspoken proponent of index fund management described in the Introduction, is a Non-Executive Director of Essentia. Yes, Charley advises a fintech company whose tools seek to improve the wares of active managers in the public equity markets. As Clare described on the show, Charley "never said there wouldn't be active managers, he said there would be fewer of them." Touché.

Cameron Hight had an insight that has helped hedge fund managers big and small optimize portfolio construction. He believed markets move so quickly that a portfolio manager cannot consider all the variables required to optimize position sizing in real time. His business, Alpha Theory, strives to make the implicit explicit by putting numbers and probabilities on position sizing decisions.

Alpha Theory uses the investment team's research to calculate risk and reward in real time. A thorough analyst already has models and probability scenarios for the potential path a stock might take. Absent new information, each movement in the stock price changes the attractiveness of risk and reward. Alpha Theory models conviction-weighted sizing based on the investment team's research and compares the result to the actual portfolio position size. Over 15 years of operation, Cameron has reams of data showing that his seemingly simple tool has added substantial returns for clients who employ it in their practice.

His data also revealed an important conclusion about many fundamental managers. Good active managers perform far better in their larger positions than they do in smaller names. Alpha Theory wrote "The Concentration Manifesto," preaching that managers and allocators would both be better served if managers focus on more concentrated portfolios of their best ideas.[38]

Summary

Data analysis almost never gives an allocator *the answer*, but the tools employed are useful in measuring risk and return at the portfolio and manager level, and in making informed judgements about manager selection.

The availability of data and the entrepreneurs at the forefront of assessing it enable CIOs to be more informed. Asking the right questions may reveal managers who eschew modern technology and are a step behind the pack.

As Robert Burns once wrote, the best laid plans of mice and men often go awry. When the most sophisticated quantitative tools land upon an outlier, CIOs need to respond. The turmoil in markets, employment, and working protocols caused by Covid-19 in March 2020 presented a recent case study for how CIOs respond to a period of uncertainty.

To learn more

Podcasts

Capital Allocators: Patrick O'Shaughnessy – O'Shaughnessy Asset Management (First Meeting, Ep.1)

Capital Allocators: Jordi Visser – Next Generation of Manager Allocation (Ep.92)

Capital Allocators: Matthew Granade – Inside Data Science at Point72 (First Meeting, Ep.22)

Companies

Novus Partners, www.novus.com

Essentia Analytics, www.essentia-analytics.com

Alpha Theory, www.alphatheory.com

Reading won't help much in improving investment results through quantitative means. Instead, reach out to Novus, Essentia, and Alpha Theory to learn more about their application of tools for allocators and portfolio managers.

Chapter 10

Case Study
of Uncertainty[39]

"Proper planning prevents piss poor performance."

– Kim Lew

Leadership and management of investment organizations is developed and implemented in *normal* market environments. Every decade or so, the markets throw a wrench in any conception of normalcy. These stressful and uncertain times put leaders to the test.

Michael Mauboussin described the psychological challenges that stress brings:

> When we're stressed, we shorten our time horizons. Precisely when we should be casting our eyes out on the horizon, we look down. And in life, people generally put much more emphasis on bad things than good things. Psychologically, between the stress or inability to think in the longer term and this idea that we tend to place more weight on the negative than positive, the result may not be ideal from an investor's perspective.

The Covid-19 pandemic that started in Q1 of 2020 provided a case study in how CIOs handle uncertainty. The novel coronavirus brought unprecedented challenges in the health and economic welfare of the world.* CIOs faced work-from-home restrictions for an indefinite period, stock market volatility, and a sudden stop in the global economy.

---

* The pandemic was sufficiently unprecedented that corporate executives used the word "unprecedented" in their communications a large multiple of any time before, and Google Trends had record searches for the word. See John Authers, "Don't Blame Me for Unprecedented Use of This Word," Bloomberg, May 7, 2020.

CIOs quickly developed a playbook to lead and manage in the face of uncertainty. Guided by their investment philosophy, CIOs created a strategy on the fly to work through the uncertain time.

Mark Baumgartner called upon military acronyms, recognizing a VUCA situation (volatile, uncertain, complex, and ambiguous) that called for an OODA loop (observe, orient, decide, and act). In their own way, a diverse array of CIOs pursued a similar path.

Each CIO first adapted to a new work configuration. Online communication became the norm across internal teams, investment committees, and managers. Investment offices tend to be small and accustomed to travel, which made the transition easier than in more complicated businesses. Full online communication was a small step away from the norm of frequent remote conversation.

Once the internal team got squared away, CIOs turned to their liquidity status. Most are accustomed to assessing liquidity on the asset side of their balance sheet, but few previously considered the impact of rapidly rising liabilities. The pandemic brought questions with unknowable answers:

- When would schools be able to reopen to students and play sports, and what might delays mean for university revenues going forward?
- With travel curtailed, what needs would a foundation's grant recipients have related to continued research?
- As hospitals addressed Covid-19, how would the fall-off of high-margin voluntary procedures impact revenues and margins?
- How would the sudden stop of revenues change the funding picture for corporate pensions?
- How should superannuation funds balance future retirement needs with the dire near-term economic hardship for its members?

The potential shock to revenues created a new variable that CIOs needed to consider before deploying capital in opportunities presented by markets.

CIOs conducted a flurry of information gathering from their managers to process what had happened, calculate performance, and assess risk. They read voraciously and called select experts in their network to get a sense of what problems may lie ahead and what opportunities may arise.

Many conversations informed and confirmed expectations. Some raised alarm bells, while others suggested a whiff of opportunity.

Big market swings provide key moments to calibrate risk and expectations. Those with proper technology and data systems rolled-up individual results and had a firm grasp on what transpired. Those without modern technology were a few steps behind. Leaning on base rates proved particularly helpful when considering future opportunities.

At the same time, experienced CIOs were slow to act. Andy Golden took a step back and wondered if he was focusing on the right things. The pandemic triggered epistemological questions about what his team knew and how they knew it. He was both proud that his team had gained wisdom from its past crisis experiences and embarrassed at having fallen short on some of the same lessons, particularly in feeling overconfident in what could transpire in their portfolio and the world. Crisis moments cause great leaders to check their ego at the door and retest their assumptions before acting.

When the time for action was at hand, allocators turned to their trusted manager roster. Absent a change in their investment thesis with the manager, allocators rebalanced by adding on weakness and trimming from strength. The most meaningful allocations went towards previously closed managers or managers with expertise in a particularly attractive area of the markets.

All these steps looked like *shelter-in-place* to anyone outside of the pre-existing portfolio. Almost none of the whirlwind of activity translated to significant action. The standard employed by CIOs at that time was *don't just do something, sit there.*

Only after the dust settled would allocators begin to focus on new opportunities. As Sandra Robertson of Oxford University Endowment Management described in mid-April 2020 after the public equity markets rapidly rebounded, "it's too late to sell and too early to buy."

When allocators get ready to turn to new relationships, they start with a prepared checklist of managers on a watch list. The list inevitably includes previously closed private equity or venture capital funds, highly ranked private credit managers, and public equity managers they have been learning about for years. Well-prepared CIOs have a shopping list ready to go when assets go on sale.

Lastly, allocators look for tactical opportunities that appear attractive when market volatility subsides. In the Covid-19 pandemic, CIOs eyed distressed debt if a wave of bankruptcies ensued, private credit if spreads stayed wide, travel and leisure sectors across asset classes, and potential opportunities in real estate once new ways of living and working got established.

Allocators never envisioned creating a checklist to manage through a pandemic, yet the sequence of events of setting internal functioning, gathering information, assessing liquidity and risk, monitoring the existing portfolio, mining the existing portfolio, reaching out to their wish list, and engaging in new relationships, became the common playbook to stay true to their mission at a precarious time.

And just as soon as the turmoil roiled markets, the markets roared back. Most of the furious activity conducted by CIOs led to no meaningful portfolio changes, but the exercise allowed them to be prepared for the next time.

3

NUGGETS OF WISDOM

Every guest on the show brings a unique story and set of experiences that inform how they invest their capital. The lessons they shared shaped the Toolkit and Investment Frameworks in Part 1 and Part 2.

In addition to these big ideas, our conversations are littered with nuggets of wisdom about investing and life. These nuggets are shared here in Part 3.

Chapter 11

Investment Lessons

Skilled practitioners develop subtle insights from years of experience in the investment process. Each has its own twist. Together, they provide a condensed wealth of knowledge.

As Patrick O'Shaughnessy said:

> No one's ever got it figured out. You have to evolve what you're doing. The best way to do that is be insatiably curious, gather as much information as you possibly can, and talk to as many people as you possibly can.

This curation of terrific investment gems is an attempt to do just that across the following topics:

- Nature of markets
- Inconvenient truths
- Managing volatility
- Investment selection
- Gaining an edge
- Asset class perspectives

Nature of markets

Investing is a blend of analysis and psychology. Managers on the show shared some of their thoughts on the nature of markets.

> "Rising prices attract buyers, and falling prices attract sellers. It is literally that simple."
>
> – *Michael Batnick*

"We're in the investing business, but it's sort of like we're in the fashion business. Skirts come up and down in our industry."

— *Anthony Scaramucci*

"Great bubbles happen around great stories."

— *Michael Novogratz*

"The market is a complex, adaptive system, which explains both why markets tend to be efficient – the wisdom of crowds – and why markets episodically go haywire."

— *Michael Mauboussin*

"It's not just the non-predictable regime shifts that cause abrupt moves in any financial instrument, it's the over-reliance on short-term market financing to underpin positions."

— *James Aitken*

"In times of easy money, a lot of stupid things work. A lot of unprofitable companies see massive increases in stock price. A lot of bad ideas get funded, and some of those bad ideas actually turn out to be good ideas."

— *Dan Rasmussen*

"A lot of things become more predictable over a long time horizon."

— *Ben Inker*

"Markets, economies, innovation, politics, weather, and everything in nature all move through long-term cycles."

— *Eric Peters*

"There are times in the markets where things are incredibly interesting. There's a lot of volatility, and your ability to add value is very high. There are other times when markets are dull, spreads aren't moving very much, and markets are not very volatile."

— *Steve Kuhn*

"If we all know what will happen tomorrow, it's not going to happen. Everybody will act differently."

– Emanuel Friedman

Inconvenient truths

Morgan Housel from the Collaborative Fund says that investing is the only field where someone with no education, background, or experience can vastly outperform someone who has the best education, best background, and best experience. It is impossible to envision someone with no education or background performing open heart surgery better than a Harvard trained cardiologist. That world would never exist. But it happens in investing every day.

Morgan's insight is one of many inconvenient truths about investing. Other guests on the show offered more.

Investing in managers

"There might only be 50 or 60 investors in the world who really can do this model well."

– Scott Malpass

"Everybody believes they're in the above-average managers. It's like Lake Wobegon children."

– Jon Hirtle

"Very few of our best investments have had every single box checked absolutely perfectly. In fact, some of our more mediocre investments had been the things that initially checked every box."

– Adam Blitz

"The Paradox of Choice profoundly states that humans are wired to want more choice and more opportunity, but the more choice they get, the more miserable they become."

– Brian Portnoy

"Most institutions are prone to overdiversification or its cousin, diworsification."

— Andy Golden

"An edge is something that can slip away very quickly."

— Kim Lew

"Good producers in almost any profession seldom make for good leaders. Money managers for the most part are highly specialized producers."

— André Perold

"Most specialist managers believe that their asset class is good, no matter what. It's like asking a potato farmer what's for dinner tonight? There's going to be potatoes on the menu at some point."

— Jon Hirtle

"Great managers, really fantastic brand-name, terrific, best-investor-in-the-world types of managers have just okay outcomes in the last five years relative to the market."

— Mark Baumgartner

"We're not willing to have 10 years where value is out of favor and have 90 per cent of our book in value managers. We just can't."

— Scott Malpass

"Asset allocators are not long-term in their thinking. There's a constant ebb and flow of ankle biters, people who come in when you're doing well and then immediately leave when it turns. I was just astonished by that pattern of behavior."

— Steve Galbraith

"If you're managing someone else's money, there's a level of either absolute or relative loss that you can't go beyond and continue to sit in the seat."

— Larry Kochard

Investing in markets

"Every time you buy or sell, you're buying or selling from somebody else just as smart, tight-fisted, well-organized, computerized, and fully informed as you are."

– Charley Ellis

"It's very difficult to get a man to understand something if his salary or management fees depend upon him not understanding it."

– James Aitken

"If you learn one thing as a philosophy student, it's that you're probably not right."

– Daniel Adamson

"There are a lot of good ways to invest, but 'buy high, sell low' is not one of them."

– Sarah Williamson

"Being contrarian means you have to be able to do some uncomfortable things."

– Andy Golden

"Baron Rothschild said about 200 years ago, 'Buy when there's blood in the streets,' but we usually forget the second half of his aphorism was, 'Even if the blood is your own.'"

– Larry Siegel

"There are limits to value investing. Ben Graham got crushed in the Depression. He couldn't resist the values. He went in early and got destroyed."

– Michael Batnick

"One of the reasons that active managers underperform consistently is because everybody's doing the same thing."

– Paul Black

"I've seen charlatans who have great results, and some of the smartest people I've ever encountered with some of the best processes who have not done well for four years in a row."

— Jason Karp

"Investment horizons have shrunk to the point that running a commercial business and being wrong for eighteen months are almost mutually exclusive."

— Steve Galbraith

"Everything is securities fraud. If a bad thing happens and the company didn't disclose the bad thing, that's securities fraud. Meanwhile, if the executives were selling stock without disclosing the bad thing, that's insider trading."

— Matt Levine

"Trends often extend well beyond what people can contemplate or imagine. If you can ride a trend for a long period of time, there's a good chance that a lot of super smart people will have gotten in and gotten out way too soon."

— Eric Peters

"When you get any type of dramatic change, no one wants to believe in it. It's hard to believe because it doesn't happen that often."

— Emanuel Friedman

"When money moves in very quickly to solve a problem, it artificially holds the bottom higher than it should. That works until it doesn't."

— Tim Recker

"Even when you know a crisis is coming, you don't want to believe it's coming so you have trouble acting. That's just a basic lesson of human life."

— Emanuel Friedman

"Correlations really can go to one."

— Andrew Tsai

"When you get a panic in markets, no theater has access big enough to handle the stampede."

— Ash Williams

"When things go bad, they can get much worse than you expect. Things can happen that don't make sense."

— Andrew Tsai

"Luck is really anathema to sports. We work hard and we game plan and strategize, and we compete and sweat. We don't want to think that this is just in the hands of fate. The same is true with investing, but luck plays a real role."

— Jon Wertheim

Managing volatility

Every allocator and most managers profess they are long-term investors. Their experience in tough times – bad markets, losses, underperformance, and stress – determines whether their intentions play out. One consistent theme from guests is their effort to dampen downside volatility to survive the long term.

"If you can soften your negative periods, you compound faster and the end result over time is dramatic. Think about it in life, if the bad times are just a little less bad, life would be wonderful."

— Chris Ailman

"I am a big believer in keeping some dry powder for a rainy day, even though I don't think investing for Armageddon is a good strategy."

— Ellen Ellison

"One of the first lessons you learn as an options trader, and the most painful lesson to watch, is gap risk."

— Dawn Fitzpatrick

"The manager of portfolios and the owner of a business need the capacity to suffer."

— *Tom Russo*

"An intolerance for big drawdowns over long time frames could potentially lead to poor decision-making."

— *Raphael Arndt*

"As long as you're not leveraged and forced out of a trade at an inopportune time, you can last a long time."

— *Jeff Solomon*

"When people are trying to mitigate a risk, there is an expensive way and a range of cheaper ways to offset negative carry. When you get a really big dislocation, people who have tried to offset that carry are often the ones who end up blowing up."

— *Eric Peters*

"Everybody hates drawdowns except for perma bears, people short the market, and behavioral scientists."

— *Dan Egan*

Investment selection

CIOs and managers also shared aspects of their selection process.

"We want to invest in managers that are driven by performance. That might be performance fees, return on their own money, or just their ego."

— *Brett Barth*

"Boutique is better, hungry is better, and having business risk is better."

— *Sam Sicilia*

"The most thoughtful investors are the ones who can distill a complex concept into an easily digestible nugget in 30 seconds."

— *Christie Hamilton*

"Know as much as you can and know when you don't know enough. If you don't know enough, don't invest because you'll never have the conviction to double down if it goes against you."

— Ana Marshall

"When you try to say, 'here's my view of the world, let's shove a mediocre manager in the portfolio to fit that view of the world', you end up making mistakes. The scarce resource is really great managers."

— Adam Blitz

"First you have to convince yourself on an idea, and then you need to convince someone else. And those require very different skills."

— Paul Johnson

"Every portfolio manager asks the same four questions: what's the upside, what's the risk, how did the market get it wrong, and is the mispricing going to be corrected?"

— Paul Johnson

"It's always two or three cards in a hand – the fundamental things about a business that matter. Part of the process is to see if Mr. Market picks up the same three cards that we do."

— Drew Dickson

"The biggest mistake in the investment business is a failure to distinguish between fundamentals and expectations."

— Michael Mauboussin

"In order to have an optimally functioning relationship between the analyst and the portfolio manager, each of them has to do 90% of the work and take 48% of the credit."

— Paul Johnson

"Deciding when to sell is one of the unheralded challenges of our business. Selling is absolutely essential when 1) you realize you've made a mistake, 2) you're offered tomorrow's price today, 3) you are rebalancing the portfolio, 4) you have more ideas than space in the portfolio, and 5) you realize a company's prospects are changing."

– Richard Lawrence

Gaining an edge

Michael Mauboussin's BAIT gives an overview of the categories that create an investment edge. Managers work hard to gain an advantage, and allocators do the same to identify a repeatable one in managers. Whether structural, cyclical, or niche, managers and allocators have their own perspective on what constitutes a competitive advantage.

"We want to find a sustainable competitive advantage through their culture, processes, and ability to adapt through various cycles."

– Sandra Robertson

"Yale has all kinds of competitive advantages. Everybody loves David Swensen. Everybody loves the idea of working for Yale. He's got this best team on his side, picking and working with managers. If you have a relationship with Yale, you know it's going to be a long-term relationship. The average tenure of their manager relationships is approximately 14 years. That's the average, even though they usually invest with people on day one or before day one."

– Charley Ellis

"The people that we think are really successful are just as hungry at age 60 as they were at age 40."

– Wayne Wicker

"Alpha is scarce and hard to find. You don't find it on the corner of Fifth Avenue and 47th Street. It may sit there occasionally, but not all the time. So you need to go where it is, where there are dislocations and capital shortages in the world."

– André Perold

"Everything in finance will be discovered and arbitraged away except human judgement."

– Jason Karp

"Active management is all about behavioral alpha: the ability of getting out of stuff at the right time and sizing up at the right time, admitting that you made a mistake and folding your hand and moving on to the next one. Those are not easy decisions for people to make."

– Jordi Visser

"If you meet a manager who teaches you something that's really new and different, then you have a chance of getting exceptional returns from that manager. Otherwise, they're all moving in a herd and doing the same thing."

– Larry Siegel

"The secret to successful active investing is to have the presence of willing, serial, repetitive or habitual losers."

– Charley Ellis

"Turnover is deadly in our business, so to the extent that you can keep leadership and strategy intact for at least a decade, that's a major advantage."

– Ellen Ellison

"What makes a great fund manager is that they are long time. They are never short time. They never give their time away."

– James Aitken

"The key is learning where to focus. Having breadth, knowing where change is going to happen, and then using research abilities to focus on that change and gather all the data points you possibly can about that change."

— *Jean Hynes*

"The farther afield you go from the mainstream, the more likely you are to find great deals."

— *Larry Siegel*

"Alpha lives in doing things other people are unwilling or unable to do. Unwilling because it's tedious and boring, or unable because of capacity issues."

— *Dan Rasmussen*

"The evidence is super clear that you must have a philosophy of long-term thinking in order to operate a management system that can operate for decades and produce world-leading performance."

— *Eric Ries*

"Our cap on subscriptions has proven to be perhaps the single most important business decision in delivering superior results to our investors."

— *Richard Lawrence*

"Through concentration and thoughtful analysis, discretionary managers can continue to do well. But if there's a data set and a quant can find it, eventually they will."

— *Patrick O'Shaughnessy*

"After Moneyball, we were taught to think that numbers are far superior to human intuition. But humans can detect things that numbers can't describe. The trick is to properly process those observations and incorporate them to get the best out of both man and machine."

— *Ben Reiter*

Asset class perspectives

Each asset class has its own set of opportunities and risks. Guests shared perspectives on opportunities and risks in hedge funds, private equity, venture capital, and a few other corners of the markets.

Hedge funds

Opportunities

"Hedge funds are the point guard on the basketball team. They see the whole action in front of them. Sometimes they put up big numbers, dropping in some three pointers. Other times they just set up their teammates and pass the ball off."

– Jim Williams

"When times are really rocky, hedge funds can be enormously valuable. When those times come along, a 5% or 10% allocation to hedge funds isn't enough for preservation of capital. The problem is allocators don't put enough money into hedge funds."

– Doug Phillips

"Successful hedge fund managers make money in very different ways, but they all have in common the inherent flexibility to go where the best opportunities sit and invest with conviction."

– David Zorub

"The hedge fund industry has transitioned and morphed. Risk mitigation has usurped return enhancement."

– Adam Blitz

"The difference between traditional asset managers and hedge funds is blurring. It's all about what value a manager can deliver above and beyond what I can do for myself."

– Dawn Fitzpatrick

Risks

"The essential skill of a hedge fund manager is continuing to run a hedge fund."

– Matt Levine

"All the gigantic multi-strategy absolute return funds are predicated on volatility scaling. When implied volatility comes down, they increase exposure to keep up returns."

– James Aitken

"Finding good macro managers is incredibly challenging because it's often hard to distinguish if someone's track record is a function of incredible skill and foresight or just dumb luck."

– Adam Blitz

"Macro has an emphasis on gurus. It's a crystal ball and a black box."

– Jonathan Tepper

"You can play the middle market in distress, but really you're on a raft on the big guy's stream. You are not the guy who creates the stream."

– Peter Troob

Private equity

Opportunities

"I was in the private equity sausage factory for a decade and I love the sausage. I think it's a really good asset class and I like what it does for overall portfolio returns."

– John Pfeffer

"As David Swensen said, the ultimate form of capitalism is private equity. You have a long time horizon, you're not beholden to quarterly numbers, you can do the right thing, and there are many levers you can pull."

– Bill Spitz

"Private equity firms with persistence are incredibly powerful businesses. They're franchises with access to deals, all sorts of levers of power, control over their suppliers, and control over their customers."

– Mark Baumgartner

Risks

"The fee drag of private equity is the biggest of any asset class."

– Steve Rattner

"You can't time the private equity market. You can't pick your EBITDA multiples because the partnerships have their own five-year investment period."

– Chris Ailman

"Subscription lines have become a significant piece of the private equity industry and represent material risk to LPs."

– Steve Nelson

"Our portfolio has no large buyout managers at all because we think that large buyouts are just leveraged equities. If there's skill added on top, and there might be, then most of the value goes away in fees."

– Raphael Arndt

"80% of deals for small businesses don't close, and that's after you come to an agreement on all the material deal terms and sign a letter of intent."

– Brent Beshore

"There are 500 companies that have been owned consecutively by three or more private equity funds. Reducing that frictional cost can have a significant impact on returns."

– André Bourbonnais

"True proprietary transactions are very rare. They exist, but they're very rare."

– André Bourbonnais

"As you pay higher prices, you get hit in private equity in two ways. First, you can't get multiple expansion, and second, you increase bankruptcy risk by taking on so much debt."

– Dan Rasmussen

Venture capital

Opportunities

"Venture always ends up on the efficient frontier. You draw the curve of an optimal portfolio and venture is always there."

– Chris Douvos

"Venture capital is important as a hedge. There's a good chance that the next 20–30 years are going to see a pace of technological change like nothing we've ever seen. If you're only invested in incumbent businesses and industries, that could really catch you out."

– John Pfeffer

"Venture capital is like Congress. Everybody hates Congress but loves their Congressperson."

– Chris Douvos

"This an access class, not an asset class."

– Jim Williams

"Venture capital has very high autocorrelation. It's just a big unfair advantage. Once you're winning, you can keep winning if you do it right."

– Joe Lonsdale

"Venture investing has this blunt tool to buy equity in start-ups. Every venture fund claims to have the same cost of capital. Some top tier firms should have a lower cost of capital."

– Ali Hamed

"A classic cliché in venture capital, would you rather have an A technology with a B team or a B technology with an A team? And it's always the latter. You want amazing people."

— Josh Wolfe

Risks

"Capital is getting very concentrated in the VC industry because companies are staying private longer and absorbing more capital. Therefore, managers are busy with their portfolio companies. That doesn't leave a lot of capacity to do new deals."

— Beezer Clarkson

"Henry McCance once said to me: When venture is working really well, time is really cheap and capital is really expensive. What happens in bubbles is that people don't have any time. As a result, their capital becomes cheap. When capital is cheap and time is expensive, watch out."

— Chris Douvos

"If you can't be with the best manager in venture capital, don't do it. Don't spend much time on it or try to find a fancy way around it, just don't do it at all."

— Karl Scheer

"There are two cardinal sins in this business. One is getting the company right but not investing enough, so that when it becomes a very large company, it doesn't move the needle. The other is the sin of omission versus the sin of commission."

— Scott Kupor

"Private equity is changing from GPs as the sun of the solar system and everything revolving around them, to entrepreneurs being the sun of our solar system where we are just one of many planets."

— Mike Mauzé

Other assets

"We don't invest in asset classes; we invest in people."
— *Tom Lenehan*

"To be a growth investor, you have to be optimistic about the future. Optimists are the ones who ultimately get it right."
— *Paul Black*

"Buying high-yield bonds is like shopping at the mall. You know what you're looking for and what you're going to buy. Structured credit is like going to a Turkish bazaar. You show up with money and you look around. You have to have an open mind to see the one valuable vase that no one else sees, and then be ready to buy it."
— *Brett Jefferson*

"If you can find an optimistic fixed income guy, I'd love to meet him."
— *Tim McCusker*

"For the average individual investor, leveraged ETFs are dynamite. They're going to blow off a toe because the structure promotes bad behavior."
— *Tom Lydon*

"Options are tools analogous to pharmaceuticals. When you know how to use them, follow the prescription, and work with experts, they can be wonderful things. When any of those things doesn't happen, they can be a bad thing."
— *Rick Selvala*

"There are 7,000 minor leaguers, and less than 10% will play a day in the major leagues. Less than 3% will actually get to arbitration and make big money. We believe that over half of the players we sign will play a day in the majors."
— *Michael Schwimer*

Chapter 12
Life Lessons

At the end of each episode, I close with a series of questions that broadens the perspective of the guest's interests and beliefs. The last two questions give guests an opportunity to reflect on what matters most. They are the following:

1. What teaching from your parents has most stayed with you?

2. What life lesson have you learned that you wish you learned a lot earlier in life?

The answers to these questions have offered a treasure chest of wisdom. What follows are some jewels across a few categories:

- Managing emotions
- Continuous improvement
- Relationships
- Work ethic
- Facing reality
- What matters most

Managing emotions

In their own way, guests on the show have expressed the value of being present and staying positive.

Presence

> "*Age quod agis* – do what you're doing."
>
> *– Michael Mauboussin*

"Don't just do something, stand there."

— Jon Wertheim

"Think twice and act once."

— Tom Bushey

"The answer will come to you; there's no need in chasing it."

— Ellen Ellison

"You're unable to control the future and the past is the past. You have to focus on right now, and you're really not even able to control that. What you are able to control is your own behavior."

— Karl Scheer

"One of the most important things to do in stressful times is calm yourself. If you can't calm yourself or slow yourself down, your fears will run away with you."

— Michael Mervosh

Positivity

"We are always plagued with our fears, doubts and insecurities. It doesn't matter who you are in the world."

— Chatri Sityodtong

"People generally put much more emphasis on bad things than good things. That emanates from this concept of loss aversion."

— Michael Mauboussin

"Take yourself seriously, but not too seriously."

— Seth Masters

"Private optimism and public despair are an interesting conflict. On one side people are quite optimistic about themselves, but at the same time are pessimistic about the rest of the world."

— Tali Sharot

"There is only so much that fits into a basket of worries. If you're going to worry about something, make sure that you have got something else you can throw out of your basket so that it fits."

— *Ana Marshall*

"You do not have to beat yourself up to be a high performer. Negative self-talk has negative expected utility in your life."

— *Khe Hy*

"It's quite difficult to not let previous things affect your future performance. And the only way you can do that is very extensive preparation and sticking to the plan."

— *Dr. Sarel Vorster*

Continuous improvement

Continuous learning and growth come with obstacles and challenges. Upside rewards await those who persevere.

Growth

"I love the Isaac Asimov quote: past glories are poor feeding."

— *Patrick O'Shaughnessy*

"Just because you're good at something doesn't mean you should do it for the rest of your life."

— *Chatri Sityodtong*

"Keep learning. Keep expanding your world. The world is a big place."

— *Mark Baumgartner*

"You don't know what you're capable of until you do something that you didn't think was possible."

— *Jay Girotto*

"Move from certainty to curiosity. If you live a more curious life, you're going to listen more. You're going to be more interesting. You're going to learn a lot more."

– Thomas DeLong

"Take the less obvious path when it feels right to you."

– Seth Masters

"There's never a perfect time for anything."

– Tom Bushey

"Sometimes a reward will only come through an ordeal, because the ordeal makes you have to let go of what you're clinging to."

– Michael Mervosh

"Walking towards something that scares you is something you always have to do in your life, even though it never feels particularly good in the moment."

– Jenny Heller

"It's okay to fail if you try really hard and give it your all. It's not okay to fail because you got distracted and you decided to quit."

– Joe Lonsdale

"Own your mistakes, let them go and move on. The faster people can learn to do that, the happier they are."

– Michael Novogratz

"Two simple rules: find a great mentor and get rid of them."

– Jonathan Tepper

Optionality

"Lucky people are the ones who try lots of things, cut out the things that don't seem to work, and continue doubling down on the things that do work."

– Dan Ariely

"As I think back on the most amazing experiences that really made a difference in my life, not one has been planned for."

— Steve Nelson

"When you can identify a directional arrow of progress, it holds secrets for you to unlock."

— Josh Wolfe

"If you don't know where you're going, any path will get you there."

— Peter Troob

"Take risks. Even if you think it's a big risk, doors open, and people help you. People want you to succeed and like to see you take risks."

— Peter Troob

"The biggest regrets that you have when you get older are not the things that you did that didn't go well. It's the things you never tried."

— Jim Williams

"Take care of your stuff, beware of debt, and time will tell."

— Dr. Sarel Vorster

Relationships

In a people business, interpersonal conduct is a long-term game. Guests offered advice on human behavior and how to build and maintain strong relationships.

"It's pretty simple. Treat people the way you want them to treat you."

— Meredith Jenkins

"Be fair, honest and straightforward in every walk of life. Treat people with respect. Work hard. Do the right things. Good things happen."

— David Barrett

"To unleash your greatness, surround yourself with greatness."

— Chatri Sityodtong

"Sometimes it is better to be caring than smart."

— Tom Russo

"Empathy is probably the most powerful skill that any person can have no matter what you do."

— Paul Rabil

"So much of what you want to do in life is build a network of people where you can add value and who can help you as well."

— Scott Kupor

"If the elevator comes to you and takes you up, send it back down."

— Rahul Moodgal

"If you have one really, really good friend in your life, you're doing a lot better than most people."

— Annie Duke

"Everybody won't always have the same objective as you, including close friends. Don't take that personally."

— Jon Harris

"Sometimes it only takes small gestures to make stressful situations less stressful and get people through difficult times."

— Michael Cembalest

"It's destructive when we make assumptions about someone's intentions. I can't know your intent and you can't know mine. We should give people the benefit of the doubt."

— David Druley

"Watch what people do, not what they say."

— Clarke Futch

"You can never be compensated enough for dealing with bad people."

— Matt Botein

"Life is sort of like one big card game. Unless you are incredibly good at reading tells of human behavior, there's a very good chance that you have no idea what cards are involved or where your hand stacks up. Play accordingly."

— Ash Williams

Work ethic

There's no shortcut to doing the work. Guests shared their perspective on what that means.

"The characteristics of the most successful people in any field are grit and perseverance. In the martial arts world, it is called a warrior spirit."

— Chatri Sityodtong

"Keep showing up, keep doing what you're doing. You'll be there when good things happen."

— Paul Black

"To the extent that you can find something that you're just a little better than others at, it goes a long way."

— Gregory Zuckerman

"With focus comes success."

— Richard Lawrence

"When there's a hole that needs to be dug, pick up a shovel and start digging."

— Tom Lenehan

"There's literally no way around the work that's required to create something meaningful with an impact and legacy."

– Paul Rabil

Facing reality

Seeing life as it is instead of how we want it to be is a common life lesson.

"People are messy, and businesses are messy. You've just got to be able to work through the mess."

– Brent Beshore

"Make peace with the mundane, because most of life is average."

– Daylian Cain

"Many intuitions we have about the right thing to do are faulty."

– Dan Ariely

"Failure is not only an option, but it's also a necessity in life."

– Clare Flynn Levy

"Confidence does not equal competence."

– Tali Sharot

"What we know sits on the head of a pin. What we don't know is the size of the universe."

– Annie Duke

"Every cloud has a silver lining, and every silver lining has a cloud."

– Jon Hirtle

"When I got a taste of financial success and status recognition, I thought that all of a sudden rainbows would form in the sky, the oceans would part as I walked, and everyone would be my friend. But instead I realized nothing about my life had changed."

– Khe Hy

"As an investor and entrepreneur, everything takes longer and is harder than you thought it would be at the outset."

— Dan Rasmussen

"If something sounds too good to be true, it probably is."

— Donna Snider

"Change isn't that bad if you're the one doing it."

— Jeff Solomon

"From Ralph Waldo Emerson, life is a succession of lessons that must be lived to be understood."

— Jordi Visser

What matters most

Keeping work in perspective makes it all worthwhile.

"All of the great wisdoms are really true: Don't sweat the small stuff; Spend time with those you love; Find your balance; Most people spend a lot less time thinking about you than you think they do."

— Beezer Clarkson

"My dad said, son, your priorities are God, family, friends, school and sports, in that order."

— Jim Dunn

"The single most important ingredient to life is your health. If you're not healthy, everything else is worthless. And if you're not happy with what you do every day, and you're not healthy on top of it, then it's a disaster."

— Jason Karp

"When you think about your kids, the days take forever, but the years fly by."

— Andrew Redleaf

"Balance is the key to life and having curiosity about the world is the key to success and longevity."

– Bill Spitz

"Time is the most fleeting of all assets. You should spend it on things that you really enjoy and where you're the most productive."

– Brett Barth

Chapter 13
The Top 10

The lessons imparted by guests in this book came from 150 conversations on the podcast.

These conversations together were approximately 150 hours long and cover 3,500 pages of transcripts.

To whittle down that work, Christopher Seifel initiated a process of outlining each conversation in a series of 25–40 quotes. His efforts, alongside invaluable contributions from Victoria Sienczewski, Marc Anani-Isaac, and Mike Dariano, prepared me to write this book.

From those outlines, I curated the best quotes from each episode. That process resulted in a list of 856 quotes that is available as a gift to anyone who signs up for our free monthly mailing list (capitalallocators.com).

As a closing to this book, I have picked a top 10 list from among those 856 quotes. The criteria are entirely subjective – each quote struck me as special when I heard it, for its wisdom, humor, or both.

Here it is: the top 10 quotes from 150 episodes of the *Capital Allocators* podcast.

1. "Anyone who thinks nothing lasts forever has never invested in a bad private equity fund."

   – Karl Scheer

2. "My new favorite bias is the bias-bias. People are now talking about behavioral finance so much, they are biased to find a bias."

   – Drew Dickson

3. "I wake up every morning saying a prayer that I'm going to pay the most in fees this year that I've ever paid."

   – Jon Harris

4. "One day I got a box with one red Louis Vuitton stiletto. The note said I got my foot in the door, can I come get my shoe?"

   – Jim Dunn

5. "Manager skill is rare. It's really hard to identify in advance. Sometimes it's hard to identify after the fact."

   – Matt Whineray

6. "Investors want to be different and the same."

   – Margaret Chen

7. "In order to finish first, you first have to finish."

   – Andy Golden

8. "One guy came and pitched me the idea of the endowment buying a cow. A single cow. I said, 'Sir, you do realize I can't buy a cow.' He went away very sad."

   – Ellen Ellison

9. "Your risk tolerance has to be the lesser of your own risk tolerance or the asset owner's."

   – David Druley

10. "Emphasize the reflective over the reactive."

    – James Aitken

APPENDICES

Appendix A
Initial Manager Meeting Outline

The following outline is an example of a preparation document for a meeting with a long-short equity hedge fund manager. It lists the topics intended for discussion without specific questions.

Background

Origins
Team
Ownership and compensation
GP commitment

Investment approach

Philosophy
Strategy
    Opportunity
    Return/risk profile
Process
    Idea generation
    Analysis
    Qualitative (company visits, calls)
    Quantitative (models)
    Write-ups
    Decision-making
    Monitoring

Portfolio construction
Hedging
Portfolio characteristics
Exposure (max, avg)
Positions (# long, short)
Largest position (cost, market)
Avg position (cost, market)
Top 10 concentration
Factor concentration
Liquidity
Turnover

Business

Goals
Team
Anticipated changes
Historical turnover
Past employees
Strategic/financial relationships
Clients
Composition
Special arrangements
Reporting

Terms

Fees
Lockup
Contributions
Withdrawals
Service providers

Investment case

Typical day
Examples
Successful investment
Unsuccessful investment

Current environment
Favorite idea
Lessons
    Learned from mistakes
    Best performance period
    Worst period

Initial meeting question list

The question list is a sample reference document for allocators to consider before entering the meeting. Bringing the list into the meeting risks getting anchored to the specific questions and distracted from the dialogue.

I. People

A. Origins of business

What is your story?
How did life circumstances shape the principals?
What is the story behind the fund name?

B. Team

How is the team and strategy built?
How does the team interact?
What norms are celebrated?
Where have you experienced personnel turnover?
Who would be your ideal partner on the team that you can't hire today?
What skills would best augment the team?

C. Incentives

Who owns the management company?
How will ownership change over time?
How is the team compensated?
How much have you personally invested in the fund?
Where is your money invested outside of the fund?
What percentage of your net worth is in the business?
What investment have employees (non-GP) made in the funds?

D. Personal

What do you want to accomplish?
What do you fear?
What was your biggest failure?
What is your superpower?
Where do you need to improve?
What do you do in your free time?

II. Investment philosophy

A. Definition

What do you believe about investing?
What is your edge?

B. Investment strategy

Why does the strategy work?
What aspects of the strategy are not replicable by others?
What would indicate your edge no longer endures?

III. Investment process

A. Typical day

What do you do when you first wake up?
When do you arrive in the office?
What reports do you review?
What meetings do you have?
How do you prioritize your schedule?
Who do you talk to routinely?
What do you do during downtime?

B. Life of an investment idea

Idea generation: Where do ideas arise?
Analysis: What makes a fully baked idea? Models? Write-ups? Reviews?
Decision-making: What is your decision-making process?
Portfolio construction: How do you size positions?

Monitoring: What do they watch? What triggers action?
Selling: How do you decide when to sell a position?
How much time do you spend on each aspect of the process?
When did you last improve your process?
How do you step back from the day-to-day and evaluate your process?

C. Application of theory

What is an emblematic example in your current portfolio?
What position is most outside of your stated process?
What is your favorite idea today?
What position are you most unsure of today?
What is the current market environment for the strategy?
What was an example of a mistake? How did you address it?
What lessons have you learned from mistakes?
What do you do differently to avoid the same mistakes?
How do you minimize bias?

D. Risk management

How do you define risk?
What disciplines/controls do you have in place?

Risk measurement
What reports do you use?
How frequently do you review them?
What off-the-shelf tools do you use?
What customized tools do you use?

Risk management
Who acts on it?
What constitutes a change in the portfolio?
What can break down?

IV. Investment product

A. Portfolio characteristics

How many positions in the book? Longs? Shorts?
What is the average position size (at cost, at market)?
What is the maximum size (at cost, at market)?

What is the minimum size (at cost, at market)?
What are your factor biases?

B. Expectations

What are your return goals?
What would an expected, difficult performance period look like?
What are your capacity constraints?

C. Landscape

Which competitors do you respect the most?
Where are you better than those competitors?

D. Track record

How does trading impact their performance?
How much is skill (alpha) compared to luck (beta)?

Appendix B
To Learn More

The following is a compilation of the recommendations at the end of each chapter.

Interviewing

Podcasts

The Tim Ferriss Show: The Interview Master: Cal Fussman and the Power of Listening (Ep.145)

Invest Like the Best: The Ace of Spades, with Eric Maddox (Ep.15)

Books

Getting the Love You Want, Harville Hendrix

Decision-making

Podcasts

Capital Allocators: Annie Duke – Improving Decision-Making (Ep.39)

Capital Allocators: Annie Duke – How to Decide (Ep.156)

Capital Allocators: Gary Klein with Paul Johnson and Paul Sonkin – Conducting Pre-Mortem Analysis (Ep.109)

Capital Allocators: Michael Mauboussin – Active Challenges, Rational Decisions and Team Dynamics (Ep.36)

Books

Thinking, Fast and Slow, Daniel Kahneman

Thinking in Bets, Annie Duke

How to Decide, Annie Duke

Negotiations

Podcasts

Capital Allocators: Daylian Cain – Master Class in Negotiations (Ep.138)

The Knowledge Project: Chris Voss – The Art of Letting Other People Have Your Way (Ep.27)

Online Course

Negotiation Mind Games, Daylian Cain,
www.negotiationmindgames.com.

Books

Never Split the Difference, Chris Voss

Leadership

Podcasts

Capital Allocators: Jennifer Prosek – Branding an Asset Management Firm (Ep.81)

Capital Allocators: Randall Stutman – Admired Leadership (Ep.150)

Online course

Admired Leadership, Randall Stutman and the Admired Leadership team

Randall and his team discuss 100 universal behaviors of admired leaders that they uncovered in their work. It is the best, most actionable set of tools I have come across. Available at www.admiredleadership.com.

Books

The Ride of a Lifetime, Bob Iger

Army of Entrepreneurs, Jennifer Prosek

It is a folly for me to try to recommend leadership books. Instead, I have shared two that struck me as being true to the lessons in this chapter.

Management

Podcasts

Capital Allocators: David "Bull" Gurfein – Interdisciplinary Lessons from the Marines (Ep.10)

Books

How to Win Friends and Influence People, Dale Carnegie

Take your pick. There are libraries full of management books. I picked this one because it had the most influence on me. I resisted reading Carnegie's classic for years because of the title. It may be the only book I read more than twice.

Governance

Podcasts

Capital Allocators: Steve Galbraith – In the Boardroom (Ep.48)

White Papers

Best Governance Practices for Investment Committees, Greenwich Roundtable[40]

Principles of Investment Stewardship for Nonprofit Organizations, Commonfund Institute[41]

Investment strategy

Podcasts

Capital Allocators: Jon Hirtle – The Pioneer of OCIO (Ep.98)

Capital Allocators: Matt Whineray – Innovation at New Zealand Super Fund (Ep.108)

Books

Pioneering Portfolio Management, David Swensen

Investment process

Podcasts

Capital Allocators: Scott Malpass – The Fighting Irish's Twelfth Man (Ep.25)

Capital Allocators: Kim Lew – The Carnegie Way (Ep.52)

Capital Allocators: Andrew Golden – Princeton University's Chief Investing Tiger (Ep.13)

Every CIO on the show adds value thinking about the investment process. I could not pick among them, so I didn't. Scott, Kim and Andy's conversations are your picks – the most downloaded shows among the CIO interviews.

Data analysis

Podcasts

Capital Allocators: Patrick O'Shaughnessy – O'Shaughnessy Asst Management (First Meeting, Ep.1)

Capital Allocators: Jordi Visser – Next Generation of Manager Allocators (Ep.92)

Capital Allocators: Matthew Granade – Inside Data Science at Point72 (First Meeting, Ep.22)

Companies

Novus Partners, www.novus.com

Essentia Analytics, www.essentia-analytics.com

Alpha Theory, www.alphatheory.com

Reading won't help much in improving investment results through quantitative means. Instead, reach out to Novus, Essentia, and Alpha Theory to learn more about their application of tools for allocators and portfolio managers.

Appendix C
Directory of Guests on *Capital Allocators*

Chris Acito, Founder and CIO, Gapstow Capital Partners

Daniel Adamson, Senior Managing Director, Wafra and President, Capital Constellation

Chris Ailman, CIO, CalSTRS

James Aitken, Aitken Advisors

Dan Ariely, Behavioral Economist and Founding Partner, Irrational Capital

Raphael Arndt, CEO, Australia Future Fund

David Barrett, Founder, David Barrett Partners

Brett Barth, Founder and Co-CEO, BBR Partners

Michael Batnick, Director of Research, Ritholtz Wealth Management

Mark Baumgartner, CIO, Institute for Advanced Study

Brent Beshore, Founder and CEO, Permanent Equity

Ron Biscardi, Founder and CEO, iConnections

Paul Black, Portfolio Manager and Co-CEO, WCM Investment Management

Adam Blitz, CEO and CIO, Evanston Capital Management

Matt Botein, Co-Founder and Managing Partner, Gallatin Point Capital

André Bourbonnais, Managing Director, Blackrock

Chris Brockmeyer, Director of Employee Benefit Funds, Broadway League

Josh Brown, CEO, Ritholz Wealth Management

Tom Bushey, Founder and CIO, Sunderland Capital

Daylian Cain, Senior Lecturer in Negotiations, Yale University School of Management

Michael Cembalest, Chairman of Market and Investment Strategy, J.P. Morgan Asset and Wealth Management

Margaret Chen, Global Head of Endowment & Foundation Practice, Cambridge Associates

Beezer Clarkson, Managing Director, Sapphire Ventures

Thomas DeLong, Baker Foundation Professor of Management Practice, Harvard Business School

Drew Dickson, Founder and CIO, Albert Bridge Capital

Chris Douvos, Founder and Managing Director, Ahoy Capital

David Druley, CEO, Cambridge Associates

Annie Duke, Former Professional Poker Player, Best-Selling Author, and Decision Strategist

Jim Dunn, CEO and CIO, Verger Capital Management

Dan Egan, Managing Director of Behavioral Finance and Investing, Betterment

Charley Ellis, Founder, Greenwich Associates

Ellen Ellison, CIO, University of Illinois Foundation

Dawn Fitzpatrick, CIO, Soros Fund Management

Gregory Fleming, President & CEO, Rockefeller Capital Management

Kristian Fok, CIO, Cbus Superannuation Fund

Ash Fontana, Managing Director, Zetta Ventures

Manny Friedman, CEO and Co-CIO, EJF Capital

Clarke Futch, Co-Founder and Managing Partner, HealthCare Royalty Partners

Steven Galbraith, Managing Member, Kindred Capital and Chairman of Investment Committee, Tufts University

Jay Girotto, Founder, Farmland Opportunity

Andrew Golden, CIO, Princeton University Investment Management Company (PRINCO)

Matthew Granade, Chief Market Intelligence Officer, Point72

David Gurfein, Decorated Marine Veteran and CEO, United American Patriots

Ali Hamed, Co-Founder and Partner, CoVenture

Christie Hamilton, Head of Investments, Children's Health of Dallas

Jon Harris, CEO, Alternative Investment Management

Jenny Heller, President and CIO, Brandywine Group Advisors

Roz Hewsenian, CIO, Helmsley Charitable Trust

Cameron Hight, Founder and CEO, Alpha Theory

Jon Hirtle, Executive Chairman, Hirtle, Callaghan & Co.

Morgan Housel, Partner at Collaborative Fund and Best-Selling Author

Khe Hy, Founder, RadReads

Jean Hynes, Managing Partner, Wellington Management

Ben Inker, Head of Asset Allocation, GMO

Ross Israel, Head of Global Infrastructure, QIC

Brett Jefferson, Founder and Co-CIO, Hildene Capital Management

Meredith Jenkins, CIO, Trinity Wall Street

Paul Johnson, Founder, Nicusa Investment Advisors

Jason Karp, Founder and CEO, HumanCo

Gary Klein, Cognitive Psychologist

Jason Klein, CIO, Memorial Sloan Kettering Cancer Center

Larry Kochard, CIO, Makena Capital Management

Peter Kraus, Chairman and CEO, Aperture Investors

Steve Kuhn, Retired Hedge Fund Manager

Scott Kupor, CEO, Andreessen Horowitz

Richard Lawrence, Founder and Executive Chairman, Overlook Investments Group

Thomas Lenehan, CIO, Wallace Foundation

Matt Levine, Bloomberg Opinion Columnist

Clare Flynn Levy, Founder and CEO, Essentia Analytics

Kim Lew, CIO, Carnegie Corporation

Michael Lombardi, Former NFL Executive

Joe Lonsdale, Founding Partner, 8VC

Tom Lydon, Founder and CEO, ETF Trends

Scott Malpass, Retired CEO, University of Notre Dame Endowment

Ana Marshall, CIO, William and Flora Hewlett Foundation

Anne Martin, CIO, Wesleyan University

Seth Masters, Retired CIO, AllianceBernstein

Michael Mauboussin, Head of Consilient Research, Counterpoint Global

Mike Mauzé, Partner, VMG Partners

Tim McCusker, CIO, NEPC

Kip McDaniel, Editor-in-Chief, *Institutional Investor*

Stephen McKeon, Associate Professor of Finance, University of Oregon

Michael Mervosh, Clinical Psychologist and Founder, Hero's Journey Foundation

Larry Mestel, Founder and Co-CEO, Primary Wave

Hiro Mizuno, Former CIO, Government of Japan Investment Fund (GPIF)

Ashby Monk, Executive Director, Global Projects Center, Stanford University

Rahul Moodgal, Partner, Parvus Asset Management

Steve Nelson, CEO, ILPA

Michael Novogratz, Founder and CEO, Galaxy Digital

Patrick O'Shaughnessy, CEO, O'Shaughnessy Asset Management

André Perold, Founder and CIO, HighVista Strategies

Eric Peters, Founder and CIO, One River Asset Management

John Pfeffer, Co-Founder, Pfeffer Capital

Doug Phillips, CIO, University of Rochester Endowment

Brian Portnoy, Author and Founder, Shaping Wealth

Jennifer Prosek, Managing Partner, Prosek Partners

Basil Qunibi, Founder and Chairman, Novus Partners

Paul Rabil, Co-Founder, Premier Lacrosse League

Dan Rasmussen, Founder and Portfolio Manager, Verdad Capital

Steve Rattner, Chairman, Willett Advisors

Tim Recker, CIO, James Irvine Foundation

Andy Redleaf, Founder and Retired CEO, Whitebox Advisors

Ben Reiter, Senior Writer, *Sports Illustrated*

Eric Ries, Founder and CEO, LTSE

Sandra Robertson, CEO and CIO, Oxford University Endowment Management

Thomas Russo, Managing Member, Gardner Russo & Gardner

Anthony Scaramucci, Founder and co-Managing Partner, Skybridge Capital

Karl Scheer, CIO, University of Cincinnati Endowment

Dan Schorr, Founder, Vice Cream

Michael Schwimer, CEO, Big League Advance

Rick Selvala, Co-Founder and CEO, Harvest Volatility

Tali Sharot, Professor of Cognitive Neuroscience, University College London

Sam Sicilia, CIO, Hostplus

Laurence Siegel, Director of Research, CFA Institute Research Foundation

Chatri Sityodtong, Founder and Chairman, ONE Championship

Donna Snider, CIO, Hackensack Meridian Health

Jeffrey Solomon, CEO, Cowen Group

Paul Sonkin, Former Portfolio Manager, GAMCO Investors/Gabelli Funds

Bill Spitz, Founder and Principal, Diversified Trust

Randall Stutman, Founder, Admired Leadership

Jonathan Tepper, Founder and CIO, Prevatt Capital

Mario Therrien, Head of Investment Funds and External Management, Caisse de dépôt et placement du Québec

Neal Triplett, CIO, DUMAC

Peter Troob, CIO, Troob Capital Management

Andrew Tsai, Founder and Chairman, Chalkstream Capital

Jordi Visser, CIO, Weiss Multi-Strategy Advisers

Sarel Vorster, Neurosurgeon, Cleveland Clinic

Jon Wertheim, Author and Journalist, *Sports Illustrated* and *60 Minutes*

Matt Whineray, CEO, New Zealand Super Fund

Martin Whittaker, CEO, Just Capital

Wayne Wicker, CIO, ICMA Retirement Corporation

Ash Williams, CIO, Florida State Board of Administration

James Williams, CIO, J. Paul Getty Trust

Sarah Williamson, CEO, FCLT Global

Scott Wilson, CIO, Washington University of St. Louis

Josh Wolfe, Co-Founder and Managing Partner, Lux Capital

David Zorub, Founder and CIO, Parsifal Capital

Greg Zuckerman, Author and Journalist, *Wall Street Journal*

Endnotes

1. Libsyn hosting service. Calculated as a rolling four-week average of weekly downloads.

2. "A Bet Against Buffett – Can Hedge Funds Beat the Market," White Paper, Ted Seides, July 2008 (capitalallocatorspodcast.com/A-Bet-Against-Buffett.pdf).

3. Data from eVestment and NEPC.

4. Adi Sunderam, Allison M. Ciechanover, and Luis M. Viceira, "The Vanguard Group, Inc. in 2015: Celebrating 40," Harvard Business School case study 9-216-026. Rev. May 30, 2017.

5. www.vanguard.com as of January 31, 2020.

6. Carol J. Loomis, "Warren's Big Bet," *Fortune*, June 23, 2008.

7. capitalallocatorspodcast.com/wp-content/uploads/2017/04/A-Bet-Against-Buffett.pdf

8. Charles D. Ellis, *Investment Policy: Winning the Loser's Game*, Dow-Jones, Irwin, 1985.

9. "Q&A: Larry King on asking simple questions and listening closely," *Columbia Journalism Review*, July 7, 2017.

10. *The Tim Ferris Show*, "The Interview Master: Cal Fussman and the Power of Listening," episode 145.

11. *Capital Allocators*, Episode 8.

12. Harvard Business School case study #693019-PDF-ENG, Toyota Motor Manufacturing, U.S.A., Inc., 1992.

13. Daniel Kahneman, *Thinking, Fast and Slow*, Farrar, Straus, and Girous, 2011.

14. www.alliancefordecisioneducation.org

15. Annie Duke, *Thinking in Bets: Making Smarter Decisions When You Don't Have All the Facts*, Portfolio/Penguin, 2018.

16. Annie Duke, *How to Decide: Simple Tools for Making Better Choices*, Penguin Group, 2020.

17. William Ury, *Getting Past No: Negotiating in Difficult Situations*, Century Business, 1991.

18. Roger Fisher and William Ury, *Getting to Yes: Negotiating Agreement Without Giving In*, Penguin Books, 1981.

19. Chris Voss, *Never Split the Difference*, HarperCollins Publishers, 2016.

20. Simon Sinek, *Start with Why: How Great Leaders Inspire Everyone to Take Action*. Penguin Books, 2009.

21. Robert Iger, *The Ride of a Lifetime: Lessons Learned from 15 Years as CEO of the Walt Disney Company*, Random House Publishing Group, 2019.

22. John Wooden, *Wooden on Leadership*, McGraw Hill, 2005.

23. Jennifer Prosek, *Army of Entrepreneurs: Creating an Engaged and Empowered Workforce for Exceptional Business Growth*, American Management Association, 2011.

24. The behaviors of leaders expressing fanness are available at: www.admiredleadership.com

25. Jason H, Karp on Twitter (@humankarp).

26. Charley Ellis, *Capital: The Story of Long-Term Excellence, Managing People*, pp. 218–219.

27. Eric Ries, *The Lean Start-Up, How Today's Entrepreneurs Use Continuous Innovation to Create Radically Successful Businesses*, Currency New York, 2011.

28. "CalPERS board wrestling with how to delegate," Pensions & Investments, September 21, 2020.

29. "Former Harvard Money White Jack Meyer Tried to Regain His Edge," *Wall Street Journal*, April 19, 2017.

30. "Harvard Money Managers' Pay Criticized," *New York Times*, June 4, 2004.

31. Available at: greenwichroundtable.org/system/files/GR-BP-Governance.pdf

32. Available at: info.commonfund.org/investment-management-for-nonprofit-investors

33. Chuck Feeney's incredible legacy is described in "The billionaire who wanted to die broke … is now officially broke," *Forbes*, September 15, 2020.

34. Massachusetts Institute of Technology, Investment Management Company, Alumni Letter, February 2017.

35. Detailed descriptions of the risk baskets are available on the New Zealand Super Fund website (nzsuperfund.nz).

36. "It is Time for Private Equity LPs to be Accountable," White Paper, August 2020.

37. Andre F. Pérold and William F. Sharpe described the conditions for the constant mix rebalancing strategy in the 1988 paper, "Dynamic Strategies for Asset Allocation," *Financial Analysts Journal* Vol. 44, No. 1 (Jan–Feb, 1988), pp. 16–27.

38. Cameron Hight, "The Concentration Manifesto," AlphaTheory, 2019.

39. This section draws heavily on an opinion piece I wrote that was first published in *Institutional Investor* on April 24, 2020 entitled "Don't Just Do Something, Sit There."

40. Available at: greenwichroundtable.org/system/files/GR-BP-Governance.pdf

41. Available at: info.commonfund.org/investment-management-for-nonprofit-investors

Index